Hands of Lent

A COMPLETE WORSHIP AND PREACHING PROGRAM FOR LENT AND EASTER DAY

WILLIAM G. THOMPSON AND PAUL E. TEPKER

C.S.S. Publishing Co.
Lima, Ohio

THE HANDS OF LENT

Library of Congress Cataloging-in-Publication Data

Thompson, William G., 1945-
    The hands of Lent : a complete worship and preaching program for Lent and Easter Day / William G. Thompson and Paul E. Tepker.
    p. cm.
    ISBN 1-556-73101-9
    1. Lent. 2. Lenten sermons. 3. Worship programs. 4. Holy Week.
5. Holy-Week sermons. 6. Holy Week services. 7. Easter.
8. Easter—Sermons. 9. Sermons, American.   I. Tepker, Paul E.,
1952-   . II. Title.
BV85.T46 1989   88-26031
252'.62—dc19   CIP

9812 / ISBN 1-55673-101-9   PRINTED IN U.S.A.

Dedication

*This volume is dedicated to the people of
Trinity Lutheran Church
Utica, Michigan*

*We are thankful that they have
allowed us the privilege of leading
them in worship.*

WGT & PET

Table of Contents

Introduction

The Hands of Lent

Lent has become in our worship life a period of preparation for the celebration of new life received in the resurrection of Jesus Christ. Such contemplation of the Lord's suffering and death quite naturally would suggest the question, "What made his suffering and death necessary?" This is a time for serious review of our thoughts, fears, commitment, and actions.

A survey of the concept of "God's hand," especially as it is developed in the Psalms, allows one a unique opportunity to consider God's activity in working humanity's salvation and how we as those who know the risen Christ are to respond to him.

"Hand" is used fifty-seven times in the Psalms alone. In biblical usage, importance is attached to the use of "hand" as part of the whole, as a substitute for a person and his activity and dealings. Thus, *the hand of God* stands for his majesty and supreme power in the affairs of human beings.

God's right hand is often spoken of symbolically, especially in the Psalms. It provides support. (Psalm 18:35) It brings victory. (Psalm 118:15) It even expresses the omnipresence of God which embraces men everywhere. (Psalm 139:10)

Psalm 110:1 is particularly significant in the light of its use in the New Testament. The king of Israel, placed by God at his right hand, is honored as God's co-ruler, one who will overthrow the enemies of God. This verse is quoted or referred to indirectly nineteen times in the New Testament.

The hand is important because our strength and energy are made effective through our hands. But the hand does not stand simply as a symbol of power. When it is linked with a personal name, it stands as a substitute for the person in heaven. The Old Testament speaks of a person's activity as the work of his or her hand. The hand is a symbol of power; likewise, it is a symbol for divine omnipotence. (Psalm 89:21)

By comparison with the left hand, a higher value is placed upon the right. (Psalm 118:15f) The left is a symbol for folly and ill fortune. (Ecclesiastes 10:2)

There is an extraordinary richness about the use of the hand in figurative language. It not only serves to express displeasure (Numbers 24:10), but also to express humble supplication (Psalm 28:2) and joy. (Psalm 47:1) Washing the hands serves not only to fulfil the ceremonial requirements of purification, but also to signify an affirmation of innocence and a clear conscience. (Psalm 26:6, Psalm 24:4) This richness of meaning, which belongs to the concept *hand* in the Old Testament, lives on and continues in the New.

The laying on of hands occurs in various contexts in the Old Testament. Hands are raised in blessing; through the laying on of hands the blessing passes on to another. In a similar vein, power can symbolically be transferred through the laying on of hands.

Also, one of the more symbolic usages of laying on of hands is observed as the sacrificer laid his hand on the head of the sacrificial animal. The meaning of this action is seen most clearly in the ritual for the great Day of Atonement (Leviticus 16), where the laying on of hands is believed to be a transference of guilt to the scapegoat. To drive out the goat meant to drive out sin itself. Therefore, if one compares the acts of laying on of hands, it may be understood that there passes to the one on whom hands are laid the particular quality of the one who performs the act.

Ash Wednesday
Dirty Hands

Text: *Psalm 24:3-6*
*Who may ascend the hill of the Lord? Who may stand in his holy place?
He who has clean hands and a pure heart, who does not lift up his soul to
an idol or swear by what is false. He will receive blessing from the Lord
and vindication from God his Savior. Such is the generation of those who
seek him, who seek your face, O God of Jacob.* *

Textual Comments:

This Psalm is possibly a processional liturgy. It may have been com-
posed especially for the occasion of the return of the ark of the covenant
to its position of honor after it had been captured by the Philistines.

24:3-6   Instruction is offered concerning under what conditions one may properly come before the Lord in
worship.

v. 3   *stand* Who may stand as acceptable in the eyes of the
Lord?

v. 4   *clean hands* One's actions should not be contrary to
the Lord's will.

v. 4   *pure heart* The attitudes of one's heart should be of
a God-pleasing nature.
Idol worship, or placing one's trust in anything other
than the true God, would also render one unac-
ceptable.

v. 5   A person of good heart and proper action God will
accept. They will come from his presence with a blessing. He will declare them vindicated, righteous.

v. 6   *those who seek him* True worship involves the earnest
seeking after God.

Sermon Outline: *Dirty Hands*

Introduction: "Don't touch" — dirty hands can make one inoperative.

 I. *To be in the Lord's presence one must have "clean hands."*
   A. The word "hands" speaks of the things we do.
   B. To come before the Lord, one's hands must be free of the telltale signs of one's erring conduct.
   C. Hands covered with the dirt of this world are not prepared to touch the clean perfection of God.

 II. *Knowing how dirty our hands truly are, we are left unprepared and burdened.*
   A. For us there are many reminders of the erring ways of our hands.
   B. What can be our hope of seeing God when we know how soiled we are?

 III. *The dirt of our hands is transferred to the Savior who assumes all the guilt as his own.*
   A. We receive vindication as the guilt of our hands is given to the Savior. (The Day of Atonement, Leviticus 16).
   B. We receive the blessing of being received into God's presence now and forevermore.

Conclusion:

We come with dirty hands, but we can rejoice that our Lord cleans hand and heart in the blood of him who poured out his life-stream on the Cross. Amen

Dirty Hands

Text: Psalm 24:3-6

Introduction:

Around my house it's not uncommon as my son comes in from outside playing, to see him running in the house just covered from one end to the other with filth. His mother screams, "Don't touch anything! Go right to the bathroom and wash your hands!" She's fearful that his dirty hands will touch the walls or some other thing and soil it. Or, he gets up from the dinner table after some particularly good meal like fried chicken, and his hands are all greasy and she says, "Don't touch anything! Just go and wash up." You begin to realize that when your hands are soiled, that renders you rather inoperative. You can't do much. No one wants you to touch anything or do anything because they are afraid that your soiled condition will contaminate them.

I
To be in the Lord's presence
one must have "clean hands"

Soiled hands are not very useful. They become a problem, and in our text they are, in fact, a spiritual problem. The question the Psalmist asks is, "How do we come into the presence of God?" He answers, on the basis of what the Spirit inspires him to say, "We come into the presence of God, or we are equipped to come into God's presence, when we come with clean hands and a pure heart." He doesn't just have reference to the fact that our hands would be scrubbed, but that our actions — the things that we do in our life — would reflect our relationship with God. His concern is that our actions would be in keeping with God's will and God's purpose, that our heart — the inner person — would reflect our relationship with God, and we, with heart and hand, would give testimony to everyone that we are of God.

However, the truth of the matter is that God could cry to you and me, "Don't touch anything! Don't touch anything because you're *soiled* and you're *dirty*." God could rightly and justly say to you and me, "You have no place in my presence." Even as God says to us, "Your hands must be clean," so you and I recognize that our hands are far from being clean. Our actions are not in keeping with God's will. Our lives, even down into the core of our hearts, do not reflect the relationship that we should have with our Lord. They rather reflect the contamination caused by our relationship with this world. Our hands have been into the dirt and the muck so much that they now show all the signs of being attached to this world.

When God looks at our hands — and, in fact, when we look at our own hands — we can see there the grime and the grit of all the things that go on in this world. We can see the marks of the gossip we speak against others. We can see under our fingernails all the grime from our scratching in the world, trying to get ahead at the expense of other people. We can see the bruises where we've swung our hand at another person without concern for who they are or what their needs may be. The bruises reflect the misuse of our hands even as we seek to reflect the will, the purpose, and the love of our God in our lives. Our hands say to us, "You are soiled," and they certainly say to our God, "We are in no way fit or equipped to come into your presence." God's quality is perfection. God is holy. God cannot tolerate that which is not holy. God cannot accept the dirt and the filth that is so evident on the hands of each one of us.

Some years ago, I had an opportunity to tour the operating room of a hospital. Even though there was no surgery going on in the operating room, just to enter I had to change clothes and put on a special scrub suit. I removed my street shoes and wore special shoes over my socks. I covered by hair with a weird-looking hat. The hospital staff made me completely cover my body so that I would not contaminate the operating room, because within the arena where they perform such delicate surgery they could not tolerate the contamination that would be brought in from the outside. That is the way it is with God. He is perfect and holy. God is the one perfect Lord who has created all things. He cannot tolerate any less than perfection and holiness in his presence.

II
Knowing how dirty our hands truly are,
we are left unprepared and burdened

Whether the rest of the world recognizes the dirt in you and me or not, it is there. And we *know* it's there. *God* knows it's there. In the great play by William Shakespeare called *Macbeth*, in the fifth and final act, two actors are standing in the shadows, waiting for Lady Macbeth to appear. Lady Macbeth enters the scene, walking in her sleep, carrying a candle. The one character says to the other, "She comes every night to scrub her hands." Very quickly she begins to scrub and to rub her hands, and she says, "Oh, spot, be gone! Oh, damned spot, be gone! Be gone, oh, spot! I can smell blood! Not even all of the perfume of Arabia could wipe away the smell of blood!" She's reflecting the terrible guilt that exists in her. Shakespeare touches the true nature of the human heart in demonstrating in her that tremendous guilt burden that she bore because of the murder in which she had been involved. The audience cannot see the blood on her hands, but *she* can. Nothing that she could do could make that blood go away. Nothing could change the spots that existed there in her mind and in her conscience because of the great evil that she had committed. Our guilt also condemns us. The world may not see the spots, but you and I do. We see the dirt and the grime, the ground-in soil of all our wrongdoings, the transgressions against our God, all that we work against him, and that which we work against each other.

We know our condition, and yet the Psalmist still says to us, "Who can ascend the hill of the Lord? He who has clean hands and a pure heart." Woe is me. Where does that leave you and me? If we admit that our hands are soiled and that there is no cleanliness there, where does that leave us? It is the message of Lent, it is the message of Good Friday, and it is the message of Easter that in Jesus Christ, God seemingly contradicts himself. This God who says that he allows no one into his presence with soiled hands, is the same God who extends his hand to you and me and says, "Come unto me, you that are labored and heavy laden, come unto me all of you that have dirty hands, and I will receive you." He invites not because he overlooks the dirt and the filth of our existence, but because that filth has been washed away in the blood of his Son Jesus Christ. That blood, while seemingly crimson, in fact, is able to purify as no soap in the world could possibly do. It is able to remove all the dirt, grime, and filth of our existence, and present us before our God as he would see us through Christ, clean of hands and pure of heart.

III

The dirt of our hands is transferred to the Savior,
who assumes all the guilt as his own

The Old Testament offers many descriptions for us regarding the sacrificing of animals for the atonement of sins. In Leviticus we read the account of the Day of Atonement, a special day in the Jewish church year, when they gave emphasis to the fact that their sins were to be forgiven. On this day a very special thing would occur. The priest would lay hands on a sacrificial animal as a sign that the people's sins had been removed and transferred to the animal. In the account of the Day of Atonement, there were two goats chosen, one to be sacrificed and one for a special purpose. As the one animal was sacrificed and its blood was drawn from its body, the blood was strewn over the altar in the holy of holies, the mercy seat, as a symbol that this blood was offered before God as an atonement for the sins of all the people. The priest would take his soiled hands, covered with blood, and place them on the head of the remaining goat, soiling its head, and figuratively placing the sins of all the Children of Israel on the head of this animal. Another priest would take the soiled goat far out into the wilderness, chasing him away. The animal would never be seen again. John the Baptizer rightly said, when he saw Jesus coming, "Behold, the Lamb of God that takes away the sins of the world." Behold, the Lamb of God — the animal of the day of our atonement, the one on whom those bloody hands were laid that bore all of our sin. The blood of all of our transgressions, of all of our wrongdoings, were laid on the Passover Lamb who was nailed to the Cross. He takes them all unto Himself and removes them far from you and me. He becomes our scapegoat, our atonement, the price paid for you and me, so that, even as we come before our Lord with dirty hands, the Lord sees not the filth of our existence but the purity of his Son's grace, imparted to you and me through faith.

In Isaiah, the prophet says, "Your hands are full of blood." But he goes on to explain, "Even though your hands are full of blood and your sins are like scarlet, they shall be white as snow." The Lord has taken our sins and has placed them on Jesus Christ. Our sins, and the filth of our existence, are as far from us as the east is from the west. Our filth is no longer counted against us.

The cry of this Lenten Season is for you and me, recognizing the condition of our hands, to come clean, to come dropping all the pretenses of our existence. Take away the mask you hide behind. Take away all the excuses you would make. Take them all away and come clean. Come clean before the Lord through the blood of his Son, Jesus Christ. Offer up your hands to the Lord and say, "Lord, I see that, in fact, they are soiled." Even as you make that admission, extend your hands to let them be washed in the blood of the hand of the Savior of the world, Jesus Christ. Extend your hand, soiled as it may be by your sins, that it may catch a drop of the purifying blood poured from the wounds of the hand that is nailed to the Cross. Extend your hand to the hand that is sacrificed, so that you might be purified in him, for the hand that is nailed to the Cross is the hand of the very Son of God who prays for us all, "Father, forgive them."

Children's Message

Note: *Consider making use of a "Pastor's Gadget Bag" in delivering the children's message. It is nothing more than an ordinary laundry bag. Whatever object you intend to use is kept in the bag until the children have proceeded to the chancel area, are quiet, and ready to see what may appear.*

Object: Bar of soap

What is this? What do you do with it? Of course! We wash with it. Sometimes Mom needs to remind us to wash before we come to the dinner table. It's not good to eat our food with dirty hands. There could be germs and all sorts of things that would not go well with our food.

Tonight, I am going to talk to you and your moms and dads about being clean as we come before God. Our spiritual hands can be dirty. God doesn't want that. He wants us clean of wrongdoing, evil thinking, bad speaking, uncaring actions and thoughts. He sent Jesus to make us clean. Jesus is the "soap" for sin. Nothing else can wash the dirt of our sin away except Jesus. During this special time of Lent, please try to remember that Jesus is the one who has come to make us clean and allows us to live with our God.

Ash Wednesday

Dirty Hands

The Prelude

The Opening Hymn *(Suggestions)*
"Jesus, I Will Ponder Now"
"The Old Rugged Cross"
"Alas! and Did My Savior Bleed"

The Invocation
Leader: We begin this service in the same way we do all things —
People: In the name of the Father, and of the Son, and of the
Holy Spirit.
All: Amen

The Offering of Our Hands
Leader: We gather on this most solemn day in the house of our
Lord. We have come, not in joy and celebration as at
other times, but in sadness and contrition.
People: We have come because we have dirty hands.
Men: Hands stained with sin.
Women: Hands soiled with guilt.
All: Hands grimy with transgression.
Voice: Have mercy on me, O God, according to your unfail-
ing love; according to your great compassion blot out
my transgressions.
Leader: You created us pure and spotless.
People: You made us in your image — clean and holy.
Leader: You formed us with your own hands;
gently, lovingly sketching each limb and feature.
Voice: Wash away all my iniquity and cleanse me from my sin.
Leader: But we have used these hands for evil.
Men: We have used these hands for murder.
Women: We have used these hands for hatred.
Voice: Cleanse me with hyssop and I will be clean; wash me,
and I will be whiter than snow.
Leader: We come to you for cleansing.

People: Wash our hands of sin. Cleanse our hands of guilt. Purify these hands for service.

Voice: *Create in me a clean heart, O God, and renew a right spirit within me.*

Leader: Use these hands for your work.

People: We dedicate our hands to you, Lord. Use them for your purpose.

Voice: *Restore unto me the joy of your salvation, and uphold me with your free spirit.*

Leader: *(facing congregation)* From this time on you cannot be the same. You have come before God with your dirty hands which have now been cleansed in the blood of his Son. Each time you look at your hands may they be a reminder to you of his love for you, in your creation, and in your re-creation as a redeemed child of God.

People: Amen. Let it be so.

The Old Testament Lesson   Leviticus 16:5-10; 15-22; (23-28)

Anthem

The New Testament Lesson   Luke 22:1-6

The Children's Message

The Sermon Hymn *(Suggestions)*
    "Not All the Blood of Beasts"
    "Just as I Am"
    "Jesus, Refuge of the Weary"
    "Room at the Cross"

The Sermon *Dirty Hands*   Psalm 24:3-6

The Hymn of Response *(Suggestions)*
    "Christ, the Life of all the Living"
    "Are You Washed in the Blood"
    "I Lay My Sins on Jesus"

The Offering

Anthem

The Prayers

The Benediction
Leader: May the Lord God of love, whose almighty hands created you, whose loving hands were stretched out and nailed to a cross, and whose comforting hands enfold you daily, now lift his hands in blessing upon you and touch you with his peace.
All: Amen

The Closing Hymn *(Suggestions)*
"Lamb of God, Pure and Holy"
"God Who Made the Earth and Heaven"
"Grace Greater than Our Sin"

The Postlude

Optional Prepartion for Ash Wednesday
(for use with ashes)

The Preparation
Pastor: We have taken time out of our busy schedules and pressing commitments to enter God's house.
We gather on this day with the family of God to celebrate God's goodness, to celebrate the way God is.
But we have come with the sign of ashes. We have come with the sign of death and destruction.
For what reason do you enter God's house in this fashion?
Why have you thus annointed yourselves with ashes?

People: We do so to remind ourselves who we are.

Pastor: And, in contrast, who God is.
All: We are but dust and ashes.
Men: Then the Lord God formed man of the dust from the ground . . . (Genesis 2:7)
Women:. . . For out of it you were taken; you are dust, and to dust you shall return. (Genesis 3:19b)

People: We do so to remind ourselves that we need to mourn.
Women:O daughter of my people, gird on sackcloth, and roll in ashes . . . (Jeremiah 6:26a)
Men: For we have brought nothing but sin and death into this world.

People: We do so as a sign of repentance.
All: Our Lord, all our righteousness,
all our good deeds,
all the things in which we pride ourselves,
are as filthy rags,
dust and ashes,
in your sight.
We can do nothing else.
We are helpless to produce any other thing.
Forgive us, as we contemplate the rich lives you have planned for us which we have transformed into ashes.

Pastor: Bear well the mark of ash.
Indeed remember who you are, in mourning and repentance.
But remember also who God is.
It is God who forgives your sins.
It is God who heals your diseases.
It is God who redeems your life from the Pit
and crowns you with steadfast love and mercy.
It is God who satisfies you with good as long as you live so that your youth is renewed like the eagle's. (Psalm 103:3-5)
Bear well that mark of ash.
But let it be only an outward reminder of
what no longer dwells within you.
People: Amen

Lent 2
Seeking Hands

Text: *Psalm 141:1-2*

O Lord, I call to you; come quickly to me. Hear my voice when I call to you. May my prayer be set before you like incense; may the lifting up of my hands be like the evening sacrifice.

Textual Comments:

Traditionally this Psalm has been regarded as the evening prayer by the church. This Psalm of David is the prayer of a penitent. The writer shows rare discernment in regard to spiritual values especially in the area of worship.

The first two verses of the Psalm could be entitled, ''An Appeal for God to Hear.''

v. 1   The opening verse shows the urgency with which the godly man would seek God's answer.

v. 2   Verse two indicates an understanding of the worship forms of the day and the true essence of prayer.

Note: ''When the Jews prayed in their synagogues, or even in the temple, they stood for prayer, probably with their arms outstretched.''
(Spielman, R. M. *History of Christian Worship*, Seabury Press, New York, 1966, p. 11)

Sermon Outline: *Seeking Hands*

Introduction: Hands can be used to communicate many things.

  I. We use varying hand postures as we pray.
    A. Today folded hands are most common in prayer.
      1. Folded hands indicate humility on the part of the pray-er.
      2. Folded hands cannot be occupied with other pursuits during prayer.
    B. Old Testament prayers were frequently offered with outstretched and uplifted hands.
      1. Uplifted hands provide an image of one seeking through prayer.
      2. Uplifted hands demonstrate an openness to receive.

II. *Uplifted hands in prayer can have special meaning for us in this Lenten season.*
   A. Uplifted hands should indicate in us an attitude of being open to God.
      1. We need to be open to God as we confess who we are.
      2. We need to be open to God as we receive his forgiveness.
   B. Uplifted hands are ready to receive the gift of God's blessings.
      1. Hands outstretched and open are symbols of faith as we ask, expecting to receive.
      2. Hands open in prayer give witness to the inner confidence of the believer while speaking to God.
   C. Uplifted hands are extended in service to God as a "sweet" offering pleasing to him.
      1. Uplifted hands symbolically point to heaven in honor of the Lord of our Salvation.
      2. Uplifted hands serve in witness to the Savior's love.

Conclusion:
   "May the lifting of our hands be like the evening sacrifice."

Seeking Hands

Text: Psalm 141:1-2

Introduction:

Hands are useful. They allow us to accomplish many things. Not only are they able to *do*, but they also help us communicate. All of us have probably been recipients of bad communications when people use their hands to make gestures that were less than complimentary. There are also good gestures — a gesture that says "hi," or a wave. In Brazil, if a mother beckons her child like this (*palm up*), the child understands that the mother is communicating for the child to come. But if she beckons the child like this (*palm down*), the child also understands that they are to come, but they are to come to receive food. The varying positions of the hand communicate to the child differing messages.

I
We use varying hand postures
as we pray

Tonight the Psalmist talks to us about our hands in the act of prayer. I would suggest to you that the way we use our hands in prayer may also communicate something.

It is most common for us that when we pray we fold our hands and clasp them tightly together. Folded hands communicate a sense of humility. Our folded hands are reminiscent of the story that Jesus tells in the New Testament of the publican going up to pray. It says, "He smote his breast, bowed his head, and knelt down saying, 'Lord, be merciful to me, a sinner.' " I can imagine that as he was bent over with folded hands, it was an act of humility. I would even consider today as we pray that folding our hands is an indication that we feel inadequate in coming before the Lord, and we are pulling our hands to ourselves, as an act of humility.

But I also know that we've been taught to fold our hands so that our hands will not get into trouble while we are praying. By folding our hands they can't be busy picking lint, or scribbling notes, or doing something else when we're praying. They are occupied in a pious way in order that our mind and heart will not be distracted during our petitions. We bow our heads and close our eyes so other things that might distract our attention from our conversation with the Lord are removed. There is good reason why we fold our hands in prayer.

But listen again to the Psalmist. He says, "May my prayer be set before you like incense. May the lifting up of my hands be like the evening sacrifice." In the Old Testament, the posture for prayer was not to fold your hands and to bow your head. Instead, it was to hold your hands up toward heaven, to pray like this (*demonstrate*). At times in very formal worship services, the pastor may even pray with hands uplifted, following the old Jewish custom. While this may not be a common custom for you and me, it does and can communicate to us something rather significant about our prayers.

In lifting up our hands, note that we have them turned open. It is hard to lift the hands comfortably up with the palm down. We probably wouldn't pray that way. By lifting up our hands in this way (*palm up*), we keep them open to receive. We pray expecting to receive from the Lord. The hand is open expecting the Lord's good gifts. It is a posture of prayer that indicates the great expectations we hold regarding all that the Lord is able to do.

II
Uplifted hands in prayer can have
special meaning for us in this Lenten Season

Very possibly we are not going to change our prayer style. We probably are in such a habit of folding our hands and bowing our heads that we are going to continue. However, during this Lenten season as we consider our theme, and as we listen to King David regarding the lifting up of our hands, it would be well for us to give consideration to the thought of praying in the spirit with uplifted hands.

When we come before the Lord with hands uplifted and open, whether physically or just spiritually, it requires an open posture. We open up ourselves. When you pray with hands folded, it appears that you've closed yourself in. And if you bow your head, it's even more as if you're folding in to yourself. It seems as if your prayer is only looking inward. But the invitation of the Lord is to come with hands uplifted. Open up yourself! We need to come to the Lord in prayer, *open* to him; open to what he is doing; open in the recognition that we come before the Lord as people who are unworthy to be in his presence. We come before the Lord open to the admission that we are sinners, guilty by our words, by our actions, by our thoughts, and by our lack of doing the things we know the Lord would have us do. We come into the Lord's presence open, recognizing that the Lord, even before we speak, even before we think, knows us and our needs. We dare not try to hide ourselves from the Lord. He knows us already.

When Adam and Eve sinned, they did a foolish thing: they tried to hide. But the Lord new their action. So it is even today with you and me. The Lord knows us. He knows us all too well. He knows all the things that we do that are contrary to his will. In spite of all that he knows about us, he invites us to come into his presence to receive his loving forgiveness. Therefore, it is for us to come to him *open*, saying, "Lord, I admit I'm a sinner. I confess to you I'm all the things I ought not to be. I can say with Saint Paul, 'the good that I would do, I frequently don't, and the evil that I would avoid, too often, that's exactly what I do.' Lord, I stand before you, open, not endeavoring to hide anything, but open before you, confessing that I'm a sinner, and open to receive the grace you've given me in your Son, Jesus Christ. I am open to receive the blessing of life and salvation that is mine, given not because I have come in such a worthy manner, but because I have come in ready admission that I live by grace, not by my merits.''

When we come into God's presence praising him with hands uplifted, it is good because it indicates we have hands open to receive. In being open to receive, we also are acknowledging that we expect to receive because we believe. We come with hands open because we believe the Lord is going to answer our prayer. Jesus himself says, "Whatsoever you ask in the Lord's name, believing, you will receive." (Matthew 21:22) When our faith is in the Lord Jesus Christ, then our mind and our will are going to be seeking the will of God in our life. When we ask for God's will to be done in our life, the Lord promises that, in fact, it will be done. When we come before him open, saying, "Lord, I can't do it alone, I'm a sinner," when we come with hands upturned and say, "Lord, I need your presence, I need your guidance, I need your love in my life," we can open up our hands and extend them to the Lord even as we ask, knowing that the Lord is going to place something good into our hands. We are never going to walk away empty-handed when we have come to the Lord open and seeking his will. It will never happen. We can extend our hands in prayer knowing that, even as we ask the Lord, he is going to give to us that which is best for our life. The Lord says to us, "What father, hearing his son request a loaf of bread, would hand him a rock or a scorpion, or something that would be harmful? If earthly fathers can give in that way, how much more will our heavenly Father give to those who ask of him?" When we come before the Lord asking and believing, the promise is that the Lord will give in blessing. We need to come with hands open to receive all that the Lord has to offer.

The Psalmist says, "May my prayer be set before you like incense; may the lifting up of my hands be like the evening sacrifice." King David is suggesting that when we come in prayer, with our hands uplifted to the Lord, this is an act of worship. It produces a pleasant aroma before God. He finds it pleasing that we would come to him. There is a good reason for God's pleasure. When we come before the Lord asking, we are acknowledging who he is to us. We are saying, "This is my heavenly Father. I can come into his presence. I can ask him, confident that I'll receive." When my children make a request of me, I feel good about that. When my daughter comes and says "Daddy" to me very sweetly, and wraps her arms around my neck, and cuddles up to me, while I know that she is coming to receive something, I also recognize that she wouldn't be coming to me unless she was acknowledging the fact that I love her and that she loves me. If that loving relationship did not exist, she would not come and ask. When we come before the Lord in a confident faith, coming in all honesty as to who we are and what our needs might be, when we open our hands and ask God to give, God feels good about that, because we are acknowledging him to be our Father, the one who created us and redeemed us in his Son, Jesus Christ. We acknowledge that we know God has given us all things and that through his Son, Jesus Christ, we can have the confidence to know that what he does for us and in our lives is for our good.

It would be good for us in this Lenten season to conclude each day with our hands uplifted in prayer, praying that the Lord would accept us as we are, acknowledging and believing that he will provide what is best for us and confident that as we come to him, our act of worship acknowledges his lordship in our life. May the lifting up of my hands be like the evening sacrifice.

Children's Message

Object: A telephone

What do you do with this?
Maybe I can phone God.

We don't talk to God over the telephone do we? No! But we do have the special privilege of speaking to him whenever we wish. We call that what? *(Let them answer.)* That's right — prayer.

Prayer is a special gift our Lord has given us. It is not hard to pray, either. It doesn't have to be much different than speaking to our mom and dad here on earth. Jesus certainly listens. He promises to hear every word we say.

I am going to talk about prayer in the sermon tonight. You help your parents listen, and also remind them how important it is that you as a family speak to God through prayer.

Lent 2

Seeking Hands

The Prelude

The Opening Hymn *(Suggestions)*
"In the Cross of Christ I Glory"
"Beneath the Cross of Jesus"
"Sweet Hour of Prayer"

The Invocation
Leader: We make our beginning in the name of the Father, and of the Son, and of the Holy Spirit.
People: Amen

The Old Testament Lesson   Exodus 29:38-46

The Sacrifice of Prayer
Leader: Just as the evening sacrifice, the lamb and grain offering, was offered daily as a sweet-smelling aroma to the Lord,
People: So the prayers of the faithful arise daily to the throne of the heavenly Father.
Men: Just as we enjoy a pleasing perfume,
Women: So the Lord delights in the prayers of his children.
Leader: I will enter your house with burnt-offerings and will pay you my vows,
People: which I promised with my lips and spoke with my mouth when I was in trouble.
Leader: I will offer you sacrifices of fat beasts with the incense of rams;
People: I will give you oxen and goats. (Psalm 66:13-15)
Leader: O Lord, I cry to you in prayer, be quick to come to my aid.
Women: Listen to my voice when I call.
Men: May my prayers ascend before you as the incense;
People: And the lifting up of my hands to you as the evening sacrifice. (Psalm 141:1-2)

Leader: Lord, you love to hear the prayers of your faithful children.

People: You hear and answer.

All: I will offer the sacrifices of righteousness and trust in the Lord.

You have put gladness in my heart.

In peace I will be able to lie down and sleep, for you alone,

O Lord, can make me to dwell in safety. (Psalm 4:5, 7, 8)

The New Testament Lesson   Matthew 26:36-46

Anthem

The Children's Message

The Sermon Hymn *(Suggestions)*
  "Go to Dark Gethsemane"
  "Rock of Ages"

The Sermon *Seeking Hands*

The Hymn of Response *(Suggestions)*
  "Glory Be to Jesus"
  "I Need Thee Every Hour"
  "What A Friend We Have In Jesus"

The Offering

Anthem

The Prayers

The Benediction
  Leader: May God our Father, whose hand is always outstretched in love; God the Son, who constantly is at our right hand to guide us and God the Holy Spirit, who holds us close to himself, bless you now and grant you a peaceful night.
  All: Amen

The Closing Hymn *(Suggestions)*
>"All Praise to Thee, My God, This Night"
>"Savior, Again To Thy Dear Name We Raise"
>"Beautiful Savior"
>"Fairest Lord Jesus"

The Postlude

```
Lent 3
Hurting Hands
```

Text: *Psalm 31:14-16*

> *But I trust in you, O Lord; I say, "You are my God." My times are in your hands; deliver me from my enemies and from those who pursue me. Let your face shine on your servant; save me in your unfailing love.*

Textual Comments:

This Psalm is a prayer for deliverance for the one confronted by struggles that threaten to consume him.

v. 14   The trust of the Psalmist is well placed. "You are my God" is both an acknowledgment of God's power and statement of the writer's faith.

v. 15   *My times are in your hands.* These words are immensely comforting. Whatever happens in my life is under the care of my God.

v. 16   *Let your face shine . . .* When God's face shines upon us, we are the recipient of his blessings.

Sermon Outline: *Hurting Hands*

Introduction: We are in the hands of God.

I. *The hand of God is the hand of life.*
   A. God creates physical life.
   B. God creates spiritual life.

II. *The hand of God is the hand of compassion.*
   A. The Scripture gives many accounts of God's compassion.
   B. God is always motivated by his unfailing love to deal with us compassionately.

III. *The hand of God is the hand of healing.*
   A. The Lord blesses us as he knows to be best for our ultimate and eternal good.
   B. Jesus Christ is the certainty of ultimate healing in God's heaven.

Conclusion:

The hand of God leads us to ultimate deliverance from the hurt, sorrow, and pain of this life.

Hurting Hands

Text: Psalm 31:14-16

Introduction:

On the ceiling of the Sistine Chapel in Rome there are two large figures of what appear to be men. One figure is a person unclothed, looking bewildered and beaten down, very much weakened by whatever conditions he is experiencing in his life at that moment. Rather limply he holds his hand heavenward. That is a picture of man, one hurting and deprived.

Across the ceiling, reaching toward this man, is another person, one with a great white beard and long flowing white hair. He has a strong arm extended down to the man. This is the image of God. The artist depicts God extending his power to man and man limply reaching up to try and receive that power. Unfortunately, man in Michelangelo's picture has not yet been transformed by this power from God because there is a gap that exists between the hand of God and the hand of man.

Indeed, when that gap exists between man and God, when man's hand has not rested in the hand of God, we see man to be limp, helpless, hurting. But the story of Lent, the message of God in Jesus Christ, is that the connection has been made. There is no longer a gap that exists between the hand of God and the hand of man. Even as man has limply lifted his hand and cried out to God for help, God in the person of his Son, Jesus Christ, has taken the limp hand of man and bestows upon him healing for his hurt.

I
The hand of God
is the hand of life

If we are to understand in a proper and biblical sense how that hand of healing works, we must understand how that hand of God has been effective in all of our existence. The hand that comes from God is the very hand of life. It is through that hand that we have life, physically and spiritually. Our bodies are a creation of God. Humanity has not duplicated, nor do I really believe that we will ever be able to duplicate, the complexity, the beauty and the potential of the human body. It is a great statement of God's creative power and the work of God's hand. Genesis tells us that God, in his own hands, took the dust of the ground and formed it into the likeness of man and breathed into that form the breath of life. It became a living creature. It became Adam. You and I are descendants of that first man. We are by-products of God's creative hand and we are the statement that God's creation is still effective in us even as he sustains our bodies.

Even as the Lord created our physical person, the Lord has also by his own hand created our spiritual person. For even as he took the simple element of the dust of the ground and formed it into a body, so God has taken the simple element of water and created in you and me a new spirit through the power of our Baptism. Through our Baptism God has granted us new life. By the working of his hand, God has created life in us both physically and spiritually.

However, if you only speak of the hand of God as being this great creative force, then you may overlook the real compassion and willingness of that hand to touch us in tender ways.

II

The hand of God is compassionate

The hand of God is a compassionate hand. If we would doubt that for a moment, all we need do is look at what God's hand has done through the person of his Son, Jesus Christ. Repeatedly the Scriptures tell us of the great compassion of God through Jesus Christ. It says that Jesus looked across the crowd, that he had compassion upon them and their hunger, and that he fed five thousand. In the seventh chapter of Luke we read that Jesus had compassion on a widow woman who was weeping over the death of her son. Jesus walked up and touched the coffin, and the son was resurrected to life. The examples are many; the Lord's compassion is obvious.

The word *compassion* actually means that "God aches for us." My nerves exist in my stomach. People say to me, "You know, you never look like you are nervous." Well, if you could see inside my stomach, you would see that it is pumping out all kinds of acids and juices. When I get nervous or upset, my gut ties up in knots. Usually my physical person will actually ache because my stomach will get so tight. My nerves are in my gut. In the mind of the people in Jesus' time, their compassion, their love didn't exist in their heart; it was in their digestive system. Just as we would say "My heart went out to them," they would say something similar to "My gut ached for them."

All of us have seen situations, especially the physical suffering of another person, that caused our stomach to actually turn over in pain for them. We may have seen someone crippled or deformed, or someone so deprived of their life-fluids through a disease like cancer, that our stomachs knotted up in pain as we looked at them. It could literally be said that our gut ached in our concern for that person. When Scripture says that God has compassion, it literally means that God's gut is aching for us as his people. God hurts for us. He has so much love for us, he aches. In God that great love is translated into action. It is in the recognition that God is the creator of our life, that God is the sustainer of our life, and that God always deals with us out of his love, that we can begin to understand how God's healing hand can be most effective in us.

III
The hand of God brings
healing to our hurting

God does perform miraculous physical healings. I have witnessed them. I know doctors who would stand up before you and testify that they have been witnesses to miraculous healings. A doctor who serves on a national Board with me told the story not long ago of a young man who had been diagnosed having a large cancerous tumor in his chest cavity. There was no doubt that the tumor was there. They had tapped it and taken a biopsy. It showed cancer. When they operated on him to try and remove the tumor, it appeared that it had all been sliced away and the tumor existed no longer. There was no cancer found in him when they operated. To this day he says there is no trace of cancer in this young man. This was a miraculous healing. And the doctor gives God the credit.

When I was a Pastor in Connecticut, I was called out of a children's Christmas service to go to the home of one of our members whose husband had experienced open heart surgery that morning. They had taken him back to surgery for the third time because they could not stop the bleeding. The doctor had called the family and said, "He's going to die. There's absolutely no way that a human being can live through this much trauma. When we take him off the respirator, he will die, and we can leave him on the respirator no longer.'' They called me to their home to pray with them and help them prepare themselves for the death which ultimately had to come. We prayed for the half hour from the time I got there until the doctor called back. We prayed fervently to the Lord that the Lord would change the course of this man's life and do differently than the evidence would have suggested. When the doctor called, the first words out of his mouth were, ''It is a miracle. He's alive.'' Two years after that, when I left Connecticut to come to Utica, that man gave me a strong hug. What seemed to be imminent did not happen. God healed him. There is miraculous healing.

But what about the people who are not healed in such a way? What about the people who continue to suffer with their infirmities, with arthritis or heart disease? What about the people who ultimately die because of cancer? Does that mean that God doesn't love them as much as he loved these people whom I described? Does it mean that the faith of the people healed was greater than the faith of these people who are seemingly not healed? *By no means!* If we could say that, we would deny that God is motivated by his compassion. It is God's love that causes him to deal with us in the way he does. That is proven, secured, and sealed by the blood of Jesus Christ. There is no doubt that God always deals with us in just the way that is best. At times that may even mean allowing some illness or infirmity that has been imposed upon us by this world and by our own frailties to continue in our body. We can't make God the author of all these evils that will plague us. God is not the author of evil, but he does promise that he can use even the things that we suffer for our ultimate good. He guarantees that through all our suffering he will sustain us in his all-sufficient grace. Saint Paul says, ''I asked the Lord three times to remove a thorn that I suffered in my flesh. Three times I asked the Lord. But he said 'no.' '' God said, ''I won't do it, Paul, because your faith is perfected through your weakness.'' God goes on to assure Saint Paul, ''My grace is sufficient to sustain you. The hand of my love, the hand of my compassion, will uphold you, Paul, so that this illness will be seen in its proper prospective, and will not bring you down. I will hold you up.''

All things that the Lord grants to us in this life are similar. When we pray for earthly healing, it is really no different than praying for wealth. Most of my life I've prayed that the Lord would make me rich. The Lord has yet to answer in the affirmative. For me to ask the Lord to make me wealthy, or to heal my body, is really not any different. Both requests are for earthly blessings. The Lord answers my earthly needs by saying, "I will give you what is best for you at this moment. I will give you what holds you closest to me." Whether that is health or wealth, the Lord is going to work that which is best, not necessarily what we merely *assume* to be the best. The Lord will give healing — physical healing — when that's appropriate. However, when that seems inappropriate, he will give the grace to sustain.

When it seems appropriate to bring about ultimate healing, God will do that. You may pray to the Lord that he would heal your infirmity, saying "Lord, remove my cancer from me. Remove it." And if the Lord physically heals, we would all praise the Lord with you. Nonetheless, somewhere down the line, tomorrow, next year, ten years from now, you are going to be sick again. Any physical healing is only going to be temporary. Next time it may not be cancer. It may be something else. But I can guarantee you, no matter what bodily healing you experience today, you are going to be sick again on some later day. That is not a permanent healing. Ultimately, no matter what kind of earthly healing you would have now, you're going to die. All of us are going to die. We're going to get sick and we're going to die. All of us. Ultimate healing comes to us only when death is eradicated, only when death is no longer a factor. Ultimate healing comes when the Lord takes us out of this life and transforms our incomplete life into that total and whole life that he has for us in his eternity. That is ultimate healing.

Some might say the Christian who dies with cancer "lost the battle." That's wrong. If we say, "his heart defeated him," that's wrong! We as Christians ought to say, "The Lord granted to him the victory over it all. Over sin, over death, over cancer, over weak hearts, over infirmed bodies, the Lord granted him the victory and gave him ultimate healing."

That's the healing that is extended to you and me by the hand that was pierced by the nail that impaled Jesus on the cross. Even as Jesus hung on the Cross, his hands bleeding to pour out blood to redeem you and me, the man next to him said in a sense, "I'm suffering. When you get to the place that you own, remember me and my suffering." Jesus, almost as if he would have extended a hand to him, says, "Your suffering's going to be gone. I'm going to heal you. Ultimate healing. The best way I can, I am going to heal you. For today you'll be where I am, in paradise.'' That hand that's extended on the Cross, the hand that is pierced by the nail, the hand that lets its blood flow freely for you and me, is the hand that guarantees to you and me that death is not the victor. Jesus Christ's victory over death is for you and me the ultimate healing.

Conclusion:

God has created us. In his love he sustains and secures us. In his compassion and great desire to have us forever as his, he holds us so near that finally it will be by his grace that we are ushered from the pangs of this world to the place where we will know healing ultimately, at its best, in God's Kingdom.

Children's Message

Object: One of the children

Want to see something really spectacular? A miracle?

Well, I don't have it in my bag tonight. It is right here before your eyes. In fact, everyone of you is a miracle. (*Ask a young child to stand with you.*) Look at how pretty this [girl] is. God made her lips and mouth that can smile so big and talk and cheer and do all the other important things mouths can do.

God made her hands and feet. God made all of her. He even says in the Bible that he made her and each of us and loves us so much that he knows just how many hairs there are on our head.

When you make things, do you like to take good care of them? Sure! So does God! That's the reason we can be certain that God is going to continue to do the very best for us. He promises.

Tonight we are going to talk in the sermon about how God loves us and takes care of our bodies, just as he takes care of our hearts.

Lent 3

Hurting Hands

The Prelude

The Opening Hymn *(Suggestions)*
"Come to Calvary's Holy Mountain"
"My Faith Looks Up to Thee"
"Lead Me to Calvary"
"For Those Tears I Died"

The Invocation
Leader: We begin this service in the powerful name of God:
People: God the Father, Son, and Holy Spirit.
All: Amen

The Litany of Healing
Pastor: As we look around ourselves we see sickness everywhere.
People: Disease, illness, and death lurk around every corner.
Men: I see the faces of those suffering the trials of cancer,
Women: "But I thought it couldn't happen to me!"
Pastor: We live in fear of crippling, life-draining diseases.
All: "O Lord my God, I cried to thee for help, and thou
        didst heal me."
Voice: *"Surely he hath borne our griefs and carried our sor-*
        rows; and with his stripes we are healed."

Pastor: Our relationships falter, sick from the illness of pride
        and greed.
People: We fight with our brothers and sisters, in-laws, and
        spouses.
Women: Friends are deserted.
Men: Relatives abandoned.
People: "He pardons all your iniquities; he heals all your
        diseases."
Voice: *"We ourselves esteemed him stricken, smitten of God,*
        and afflicted; and with his stripes we are healed."

40

Pastor: Our relationships with our Lord suffer from our sin-sickness.
People: Sometimes we feel so far from you, Lord.
Men: How can I even show my face before Him?
Women: How could he still love me after I did that?
People: "My God, My God, why hast thou forsaken me?"
Voice: *"He was wounded for our transgressions; and with his stripes we are healed."*

Men: "O my God, I cry by day but thou dost not answer;"
Women: "And by night, but I have no rest."
Voice: *"He was bruised for our iniquities; and with his stripes we are healed."*

Pastor: Heal us, O Lord.
People: Heal us, by your Word.
Voice: *"The chastisement of our peace was upon him; and with his stripes we are healed."*

Pastor: "The Lord sent his Word and healed them."
All: "And with his stripes we are healed."

The Old Testament Lesson   Isaiah 53:1-6

Anthem

The New Testament Lesson   Luke 22:47-53

The Children's Message

The Sermon Hymn *(Suggestions)*
        "Grant, Lord Jesus, that My Healing"
        "I Love to Tell the Story"
        "Jesus, Thy Blood and Righteousness"

The Sermon *Hurting Hands*   Psalm 31:14-16

The Hymn of Response *(Suggestions)*
        "Drawn to the Cross, Which Thou hast Blest"
        "Be Still, My Soul"
        "There Is a Balm in Gilead"

The Offering

Anthem

The Prayers

The Benediction
    Pastor: May the God of power and might now go with you;
              May he uphold you in his strong hand;
              May he guide you with his ever-watchful eye;
              And heal you with his gentle touch of peace.
    All: Amen

The Closing Hymn *(Suggestions)*
      "Abide With Me"
      "Nearer, My God, to Thee"
      "The Blood Will Not Lose Its Power"

The Postlude

Lent 4
Nervous Hands

Text: *Psalm 139:1-6*

O Lord, you have searched me and you know me. You know when I sit and when I rise; you perceive my thoughts from afar. You discern my going out and my lying down; you are familiar with all my ways. Before a word is on my tongue you know it completely, O Lord. You hem me in, behind and before; you have laid your hand upon me. Such knowledge is too wonderful for me, too lofty for me to attain.

Textual Comments:

The Psalmist offers a meditation full of feeling as he considers God's omnipresence. He writes very personally, acknowledging God's full awareness of who he is, what he does, and all of his needs.

v. 5   *You hem me in . . .* The believer here writing is awed that no matter where he turns he is in God's power.

. . . you have laid your hand upon me. God has taken the initative to designate this individual as his own. He blesses him through his presence.

Sermon Outline: *Nervous Hands*

Introduction: One is usually nervous because of fear.

I. The fears of our life can cause us to have nervous hands.
   A. A variety of fears may cause our concern.
      1. Some fear failure.
      2. Some fear the unknown of the future.
      3. Some fear rejection.
   B. In the account of Jesus' passion, we can observe the nervous hands of Peter. (Matthew 26:69-75)
      1. Peter was afraid to appear weak.
      2. Peter's own self-fears allowed him to betray his Lord.
      3. We are similar to Peter: our fears often produce unwanted actions.

II. *The loving touch of our God calms our fears and quiets our nervous hands.*
   A. God knows everything about us and what is needed to remove our fears.
      1. He knows our fears and needs.
      2. He knows the inmost parts of our being.
      3. He has "laid his hand" on us through faith.
   B. God is present everywhere; his love surrounds us.
      1. Nothing can separate us from the presence of God.
      2. ". . . Your right hand will hold me fast" (v. 10) is God's promise to us.

Conclusion:
   The touch of God's loving hand secures us in the face of our fears.

Nervous Hands

Text: Psalm 139:1-6

Introduction:

All of us at some point have been so nervous that it was obvious to everyone — our knees shook, our hands trembled. It's happened to every one of us. I remember one incident in particular in my own life. It was the first time I ever assisted with Communion. I was a Lay Minister. It was my installation, and I was to assist in distributing Communion. My hands shook so badly in trying to pass out the bread that I'm quite certain that everyone who received a wafer had to shake his head to catch my hand. I was trembling because I was afraid. That's what nervousness really is. Nervousness is not something that exists in itself; it is a symptom of being afraid. You and I have had a lot of fears in our lives causing nervous hands.

I
The fears of our life
can cause us to have nervous hands

Whether our hands actually tremble or not, we know that inside of us there is a lot of trembling, because there are all kinds of fears. We are afraid to fail. We are afraid that something is going to be presented to us that we cannot accomplish. We admit, "I'm afraid." Our fear may even cause us to retreat from new adventure. "I can't do it," we say. We are introduced to a new machine in the office and we look at it and say, "Oh, I can't do that. I'll never figure that out. I don't want any part of it." Or, we look at some new event or some new change in our life and say, "Oh, I'll never, never be able to handle that. I don't want to go to a new school. I don't want to go to a new job. I might not be able to make it there. I'm comfortable in my own little niche." We are afraid of the things that might challenge us, fearful that with the challenge we will not be up to it, and we will fail. It makes us nervous.

We are afraid of the unknown. We are afraid of the things that lurk beyond our understanding or loom in the dark. All of us are afraid of the dark. Every one of us. That's why night lights are sold at every department store. We don't like the darkness. We are all smart enough to say that the darkness is not going to reach out and grab us. It is not the darkness that grabs us, but there is always that haunting fear of what is hidden in the darkness. You go in your own room at night. You know what that room looks like. You know where everything in that room is located. When the light is on you are very comfortable. When the light is off, nothing in that room is changed, but all of a sudden you're afraid. You're afraid, because you don't know what else has been introduced into that room since the lights have gone out. Maybe something will reach out and grab you. The darkness makes us afraid because we don't know what is lurking there. We don't know what's to come. We don't know what's around the corner. We don't know what tomorrow will bring. Those unknowns make us nervous because we're afraid of them.

When I was a boy growing up, my house was located about a block and a half off the main thoroughfare. If I went anywhere of any distance at night, my friends and I would take the bus. The bus let off at the corner and I would walk home alone in the dark. Now you have to realize that all of my life I lived on the same street. My parents still live on that street. I knew that street perfectly well, but at night it was different. The street was lined with large oak trees whose limbs hung over the street. About every third of a block there was a street light. The street light played all kinds of tricks as it shone through the limbs of the trees. The street that I was walking down was a street that I knew, but in the darkness it could be scary. I could hear dogs bark, see movement in the bushes, detect lights flickering across the pavement. In the darkness I didn't know what danger might be out there. I was afraid.

Whether you're a child, a teenager, or maybe even more when you are an adult, a fear exists in you as you question, "What will tomorrow bring?" What will tomorrow's check-up at the doctor bring? A disease? An illness? What will the audit by the IRS bring next week when they look at my income tax? What will tomorrow bring when my auto has to go in for repairs? What does tomorrow bring when I look at a new job, or graduate from the eighth grade and go to high school, or graduate from high school and go to college? Whatever I do, what will tomorrow bring? It is an unknown. It makes us nervous because we're afraid.

We are afraid of being rejected. A lot of things we do in our life are done in order that people will affirm us. We want others to say, "You're all right. I like you." We don't want to hear people say, "I don't like you." We are afraid of rejection. It makes us nervous to think we are not going to be accepted by others. To be certain that we will be accepted, so that our fears will be set aside, we do all kinds of things to put ourselves into what we think is the right position to remove the threat. We try and build secure lives that don't change so we don't have to deal with change. We try to guarantee tomorrow, arranging it just the way we want it. We perform for each other so that others will affirm us. Our hope is to eradicate our fears, so that we don't have to be nervous about life.

In the Scripture story of Jesus' trial, there is an example of a man whose fears are easily seen. He's standing around the fire outside of the high priest's home and he's afraid. However, this is not the first demonstration of fear that we see in Peter. Peter is afraid even as he boasts. Jesus says, "They're going to take me and crucify me." Peter says, "It will never happen, not as long as I'm around. I'll take care of you. It'll never happen." There is a fear in him, the fear that the Lord would say, "Aren't any of you going to support me?" I can just imagine that even then Peter's hands were trembling. "O Lord," he says, "I'll be right there with you all the way." He was ready to boast for the moment so that he could gain other's approval. But only hours later, due to a new fear, he was willing to deny the Lord. He was nervous when he thought his own hide was in jeopardy. When it came time for Peter to be approved by the crowd, he was willing to give up the Lord because of his own fear. That's exactly what happens to you and me, as too frequently fear becomes a motivator in us. Fear becomes the motivation in us that causes us to do things that are not in keeping with our relationship with the Lord. It is a real basic problem in Peter, a problem that you and I share. If you go back and read Peter's big boasting, that "If they come and take you, Lord, I'll be there," you begin to realize that Peter's biggest problem was that he was too self-reliant. He was dependent upon himself. He stood up and said, "Lord, I'll protect you, I'll do it, I can withstand it, I can draw my sword out and I can cut off the man's ear. I can do it, Lord. I can do it." But when the *I* had to do it, it failed.

If you and I depend only upon ourselves, if we are totally self-reliant, we have good reason to be afraid. We have good reason to tremble in the face of our own existence. If we rely only upon ourselves, then we are relying upon someone who is frail, on someone who frequently fails, on a person who has proven that he or she is not totally reliable. If we rely only upon ourselves, we are building our security on someone whom we know will eventually pass away. Self-reliance cannot work; consequently, there's a reason to be afraid.

II

The loving touch of our God calms our
fears and quiets our nervous hands

Go back with me to the Psalm. Hear the message of comfort, a message that existed in the time of Jesus Christ, a message that he brought through his preaching and a message that still exists for you and me today. Listen again as the Psalmist records these words and gives us great comfort in the face of our fears. "O Lord, you have searched me and you know me, and you know when I sit down and when I rise up; you perceive my thoughts from afar. You discern my going out and my lying down; you're familiar with all of my ways." In one sense, that is somewhat frightening in itself, that the Lord knows all of our ways and all of our thoughts. The Lord is well aware of all of our fears. Yet, the Psalmist says that the Lord, in knowing all of our fears, still cares for us. "You know it completely, O Lord, and you hem me in behind and before; you have laid your hand on me. Such knowledge is too wonderful for me, it's too lofty for me to even think about." "You have laid your hand on me" — that's the testimony of the Psalmist, that the Lord in his knowledge of who we are has touched our lives with his grace. He knows our needs, our fears, and our frailties. In spite of all of that, he still loves us. When we walk down the dark roads of our existence, or we are faced with all the things that cause our hands to tremble and our knees to knock, the Lord is still there.

Your faith is testimony to you that the Lord has laid his hand on you. Through the waters of your Baptism the Lord has known you. You are not merely a number to the Lord. You're not something that "just exists" in the world. Instead, you are known by the Lord. You are known personally by the Lord, and he knows everything about you — all of your needs and all of your weaknesses. He understands all the fears that rise up out of those needs and those weaknesses. Your faith is testimony to you that in knowing all about you, the Lord is still interested in being in your life. The Lord is eager to have you as his. The Lord wants you to live in the certainty that you've been called to be his child.

"The Lord has laid his hand upon me," the Psalmist says. "Such knowledge is too wonderful for me.'' How beautiful! Not only does the Lord know us, but the promise that the Psalmist proclaims is the very promise that Jesus himself gives in the concluding words of the Gospel of Matthew: "Lo, I am with you always, even unto the end of the age.'' We are never alone. We never stand alone in fear against the world. No matter where we go, the Lord is there. It is easy when you and I are in this church to feel that the Lord is with us. When we are sitting with our Bible in our lap and reading; when our minds are set on those heavenly things, it's easy to believe that the Lord is with us. But the Psalmist says, "If I make my bed in the depths, you are there.'' Your life may seem to you to be nothing but a deep pit. But there is no pit in this world so deep, there is no depression, there is no fear, there is no existence, there is no torment, there is no pain, there is nothing in this world that can be so deep that the Lord cannot come and find you and me and lift us out. There is no place in this world that can bar you from the grace of God. There is no fear that need overcome you. You know the Lord who enters the depths of our existence to be near us, to take us by the hand and guide us to a greater awareness of his grace and the life that is ours in him.

On more than one occasion I have sat at a sickbed, a deathbed, or a coffin. I have sat with a parent lamenting the misconduct of a child. I have watched people hurt and be so upset that their hands literally trembled. I have experienced people so distraught over the situation in their life, that they literally shook in fear. To try and reassure them that someone cared and someone was there to support and encourage them, I frequently have taken their trembling hands in mine and held them firmly. It is just a means of saying to them, "You know, I care about you. The Lord cares about you. It's going to be better.'' It is a very small gesture, but it seems to help. The Scripture is telling us that the Lord has reached out with the nail-pierced hands of his Son to calm our nervous hands. Hands that are strong yet loving, hands that are mighty yet caring, hands that have been pierced by the nails of the Cross, are extended to you and me. Reassuring hands reach for us in faith, that being touched by his grace we might understand his promise — the promise that allows us to hear our Lord say, "You are loved; there is nothing, no fear, no problem, no pit so deep, nothing that can snatch you out of my hand.'' That's the Lord's promise to you and me. May it be your comfort, your strength, and your security now and forever.

Children's Message

Object: Child's night light

What is this? Do most of you have one in your home? Why?

It is a night light. It helps us see in the dark. In our house we use them when we go to bed so in case we need to get up, the light will help us see in the dark. I like having a light like this. With a light I am not afraid of the dark.

Did you know that the Bible says Jesus is a light? He is the Light of the world. He is a light for us so we don't have to be afraid. He promises always to be with us. He tells us nothing can take us away from his love.

We don't always know what is going to happen next. Sometimes we are sick, or our parents are sick, or maybe our grandparents. Jesus comes in his love as a light to us to let us see that nothing — not sickness nor anything else — can take us away from him.

Tonight in the sermon, we are going to talk about the truth that Jesus is always with us; therefore, we don't have to be afraid.

Lent 4

Nervous Hands

The Prelude

The Opening Hymn *(Suggestions)*
"Christ, the Life of All the Living"
"In the Cross of Christ I Glory"
"I Know a Fount"

The Invocation
Pastor: We begin our worship in the name of the Triune God:
All: God the Father, God the Son, and God the Holy Spirit.
         Amen

The Old Testament Lesson   Psalm 139:1-12

The New Testament Lesson   Matthew 26:69-75

The Conversation
Pastor: Like Peter, sometimes I have nervous hands;
Women: Hands that shake;
Men: Hands that break out in cold sweat;
People: Hands that betray my inner feelings of fear.
Pastor: Fear of what people may think.
Men: Fear of what others might say.
Women: Fear that I may be ridiculed in front of my friends.
Pastor: Sometimes my nervousness is because of sins that I have
        done.
People: Sometimes it is because of hasty words that I have said.
Pastor: Like Peter, I might wring my hands;
People: Like him I may try to hide my nervousness.
All: But it always shows through.
Pastor: There are even times when, like Peter, I am nervous and
        afraid to let others be aware that I know the Lord.
Women: Sometimes it is just more convenient to not mention that
        I am his child.

Men: But that isn't really the same as denying that I know him. Is it?

Voice: I know we're not twenty-one yet, but I was told of a place where we can pick up a case.

People: Is it really wrong to say nothing?

Voice: We can put one over on the boss if we just claim that we actually worked those extra hours.

Men: But I'd be laughed at if I said anything. Who's going to be hurt by it anyway?

Voice: Aw, come on! You don't mean to tell me that you really believe in that "Jesus" stuff?

Women: I think it's all right to say nothing as long as no one asks.

Voice: I just did.

Pastor: "And Peter remembered the words of Jesus . . . and he went out and wept bitterly."

All: Lord, grant me the strength and power to overcome nervousness — nervousness of sin and guilt; nervousness to speak up and admit that I know you. This I ask in Jesus' name. Amen

Anthem

The Children's Message

The Sermon Hymn *(Suggestions)*
    "In the Hour of Trial"
    "There Is a Fountain Filled With Blood"
    "Anywhere With Jesus"

The Sermon *Nervous Hands*   Psalm 139:1-6

The Hymn of Response *(Suggestions)*
    "Alas! and Did My Savior Bleed"
    "Because He Lives"
    "Jesus Walked This Lonesome Valley"

The Offering

Anthem

52

The Prayers

The Benediction
Pastor: We conclude with the blessing of the Lord:
All: May the Lord, whose powerful hands formed us of earth, whose loving hands were bound as he was tried for our sins, and whose mighty hands encourage us daily, grant us now his peace. Amen

The Closing Hymn *(Suggestions)*
"We Sing the Praise of Him Who Died"
"Jesus, Lover of My Soul"
"Lord, Take My Hand and Lead Me"

The Postlude

Lent 5
Angry Hands

Text: *Psalm 26:5-6*
> *I abhor the assembly of evildoers and refuse to sit with the wicked. I wash my hands in innocence, and go about your altar, O Lord.*

Textual Comments:

David, as he writes this Psalm, is apparently disturbed and angry, due to the false accusations that are being made against him. He prays for vindication and protection from these evildoers.

v. 5   The Psalmist first clarifies that he does not associate with the wicked. He strives for positive, God-fearing relationships.

v. 6   Aside from avoiding deceitful men, the writer aims to preserve a proper conduct. "I wash my hands in innocence . . ." reflects the ritual of hand washing as a sign of guiltlessness.

go about your altar . . . To praise God at his altar for his saving work was an act of devotion.

Sermon Outline: *Angry Hands*

Introduction: Anger can be an appropriate response, or it can be destructive and vicious.

I. Anger can be misdirected, and therefore an improper and negative force.
  A. Anger is a natural emotion, and at times it is appropriate.
  B. However, much of our anger is misdirected and inappropriate.
  C. Misdirected anger is a negative force. The Christian should be seeking the positive.

II. Anger for the Christian should be seen in the light of God's mercy and controlled by the power of God's Spirit.
  A. The Christian's calling encourages him to deal with life and its emotions in a manner that reflects the Lord's presence.

      1. Anger surrounds the Christian in today's world.
      2. The agony of Lent is a reminder of the anger of evil people turned toward the Savior.
  B. How can we best praise our God in the face of anger?
      1. When challenged by anger, we need first to turn the matter over to the Lord in prayer.
      2. Secondly, we should question our anger. Is sin involved, or is my anger misdirected?
      3. Upon recognizing the cause of our anger, we should ask, "What response is appropriate for me as a Christian?"
      4. Finally, as the redeemed of God, we need always to seek to forgive as we have been forgiven.

Conclusion:

May the love of our Savior dispel our anger, that we might serve him in joy.

Angry Hands

Text: Psalm 26:5-6

Introduction:

When we review the images of Lent, our theme of "Angry Hands" is not hard to visualize. One can well imagine that fists were clenched and raised as on Good Friday the crowd shouted "Crucify him, crucify him!" The angry hands of Roman soldiers struck Jesus' face, mocking and ridiculing him. Their anger was directed against the one who came to show them all God's love. What a mistake! Too frequently such misdirected anger is still evident in the way we deal with one another and in the manner in which we deal with God.

I
Anger can be misdirected, and therefore
an important and negative force

Some years ago I was playing golf with a man who I knew had a pretty strong temper, but I didn't realize quite how bad it was. We were on one of the final greens. He missed a putt. All of a sudden he tried to wrap his putter around a tree. What misdirected anger! It was so poorly directed, it did not make sense. It was not the inanimate piece of metal that had missed the putt, but the individual holding the putter. Never should anger be so wrongfully directed. It is misdirected anger when we turn our vengeance against those which have no part or parcel in the problem.

I have to admit to you that at times in my life I have even shouted at God, "God, why in the world have you *done* this? I'm *angry* with you, God!" I have been angry with God when I saw things that I thought were unjust and wondered why they were allowed. I've been angry with God when situations didn't develop as I thought they should. I've been angry with God when I have had to participate in the burial of the young, or others who I thought died at an inappropriate time. I have been angry with God. But that, too, is misdirected anger. It is an anger that makes no more sense than the man who wrapped his putter around the tree. It is not the putter that did it, and it is not God who works the evil in our life. It is the world in which we live, and the weakness of us who live here.

The Psalmist prays that the Lord would redeem him and remove him from those who in their hands scheme against him and those who in their right hands hold bribes that would work against him. God has not desired that any person would die. Why would I be angry with God? God didn't do it. The sin that humanity commits brought death into the world. God didn't. The evil that is worked in our lives is too frequently due to our evil and our doing. It is not God's. God's promise is to bring the good out of it, to hold us in his hand so that we can overcome that evil. It is misdirected anger if our anger is directed toward our God.

However, some anger is good. Some anger is proper and right. Some anger is natural. If we didn't release some of it, we would explode. The Bible tells us that God was angry. God doesn't sin. There would have to be proper and righteous anger. In the Gospels we are told that Jesus caused the fig tree to wither. That was a proper anger. The fig tree did not produce as God created it to do. There is even righteous anger among you and me today when we rightly direct our vengeance of our wrath against that which is truly wrong, against the sin and not against those things that have no part nor any cause in it. One good example of what I believe is a righteous anger today is an organization that was formed by a group of angry mothers. It is called Mothers Against Drunk Drivers. They are mothers who have lost children or have had children severely injured in accidents which involved people who were drinking and driving. That is a righteous anger. Those mothers have a right to be angry with the sin.

If we're going to look at God's example and strive to follow God's pattern, we will observe that God in his righteous anger directs that anger properly. He directs his anger at that which is wrong and not at those who fall prey to the wrong. Our anger is too often misdirected. We don't direct it at the wrong, but we direct it at ourselves and we direct it at the people who are around us, who are only victims of that wrong.

In the passion account we see anger. The Scribes, the Pharisees, and the Sanhedrin are angry at Jesus because he is attracting the people. However, they did not have the good sense to look into their lives and search for the source of that anger. They rather directed it at the thing that they most wanted to do away with, Jesus Christ. Possibly if the Sanhedrin would have considered for a moment their anger, they would not have crucified Jesus Christ. Rather, they would have revered, praised, and worshiped him as the King and Lord of their salvation. But in their anger, in their misdirected anger, they visited upon him all of their wrath, hoping that the problem would go away. But it didn't. It didn't change a thing. All their scheming didn't make Jesus Christ go away. The Sanhedrin in all of their anger sought to destroy the Lord of their salvation. They were the losers.

II
Anger for the Christian should be seen in the light
of God's mercy and controlled by the power of God's Spirit

As Christians, we often picture life in this world as a broad road leading to destruction. We see the Christian life as a narrow path that leads to glory. The illustration may be accurate. However, that narrow path is not a separate road. In fact, it is laid right down the very middle of that broad path, but it runs in the opposite direction. As the great throngs of people are coming down that broad road, the Christian is walking the narrow path down the middle of that crowd, going the opposite direction. I don't know if you have ever tried to walk against the flow of the crowd in a busy mall or athletic arena. If the people are trying to leave, and for some reason you are endeavoring to enter, it is practically impossible. Our walk in this world against the flow could try your patience. The world wants you and me to be angry. When we look around us, we discover that there are a lot of things to provoke anger in us. There is destruction, there is injustice, there is poverty and war. There are many things that are obviously contrary to the way that God would have them.

Unfortunately our anger is too frequently misdirected and misapplied. Satan wants us to take our anger and use it to cloud our thinking. His desire is for us to use our anger against each other — spouse against spouse, children against parents, neighbor against neighbor. The devil wants to turn our anger to violence, violence like that visited upon Jesus Christ. In no way can such anger be pleasing to our God. In no way can such violence be in keeping with any notion of a righteous or a proper anger. Lent demonstrates to you and me in graphic ways what misdirected, inappropriate anger can do. It killed the very Son of God.

However, out of Jesus' death God has brought you and me blessing. Out of that misdirected anger, God has given to you and me life and salvation. As the anger of the world was visited upon Jesus

Christ, he took upon himself our pain and our suffering, that such anger would not destroy us, even as it was intended to destroy him. It is Christ, the one who suffered all the wrath of this world's anger, who calls to you and me today. He calls for us to look at our lives and our living in new ways. He calls for us not to direct our anger toward each other, but rather, direct it toward the sin and the corruption that works against us, our relationships with each other, and our life with God.

The Psalmist concludes, "Allow my feet to stand on level ground." What Jesus Christ did in giving himself at Calvary is the answer to the Psalmist's prayer. It is the answer to our prayer. It is the answer to our prayer that God would consume our anger and take it out of us, asking him to remove all the bitterness that exists in us, all the scheming that we do against each other gossiping and back-stabbing, seeking his release from all the other things that are so prevalent in us as human beings, even in Christian human beings, praying that he would remove our anger and we would seek a more positive life.

While anger may be natural to you and me, anger is a negative emotion. We as Christians need to be talking about the positive, the building, the affirming, not that which tears down. "Let my feet stand on level ground," says the Psalmist. I would like to suggest to you on the basis and by the power of God something that I believe you can do that is positive in regard to how you deal with anger. How does a Christian deal with anger? You begin by praying to the Lord, "Let my feet stand on level ground." Recognize that we stand levelly and firmly in the love of our Lord and Savior Jesus Christ. That is the positive in our life, not the negative. That is the beginning point.

Secondly, when anger rises up in you, take just one moment to ask yourself the question, "Why am I angry? What is it that is making me so mad? Is it the fact that I'm embarrassed by the situation? Is it that I'm tired and my children are getting on my nerves? Is it that I'm threatened by a situation in my life that I'm afraid? Is anger serving as a way for me to cover over my fear? Or, is it that I see a sign with which I am unhappy and displeased and therefore rightly angered? Why am I angry? Is there a sin involved in that which angers me?" If there is no sin, then our anger is misdirected. Once we have taken that moment to identify the source of our anger and we recognize why it is there, then we need to remember that appropriate anger is directed toward sin. If we are angry with sin, that's a righteous anger. If we see the source of that anger to be something other than sin, it is misdirected anger.

"What, then, is appropriate? What is appropriate for me to do?" If it is misdirected anger, it is appropriate for us to fall on our knees and ask the Lord to forgive us, to calm us, and to restore us. If it is a properly directed anger, we need to say, "God, what would you have me to do?", at the same time asking God for direction. Also, we can ask of ourselves, "How would I like to be treated?" If someone was angry with me, rightly or wrongly, how would I want to be treated?

Finally, we need to live continually in the knowledge that we are forgiven people. We are not righteous people by our own merit, but forgiven people, declared righteous through Jesus Christ, forgiven by the blood of the Savior, wiped clean of our sins by him who knew no sin and gave his life up for us. We are forgiven, redeemed children of God and, being such, we need to have the highest motivation to forgive one another even in the midst of our anger. We are to forgive even as we have been forgiven.

During this Lenten season, when we see the raised angry hands of those who are crying, "Crucify him, crucify him," when we see the anger of all the things that surround us in this world, may we recognize that anger in our lives is too frequently misdirected. May it be our desire as God's people to live the positive, Christ-filled life. Allow Christ to lead you on that path. Lift up your hands in prayer and let the Savior take your hand and lead you beyond all the negatives of this world, to walk in the positive aspects of his grace, knowing that anger has been wiped away by the forgiving love of the Savior, Jesus Christ.

Children's Message

Object: Flashlight without batteries inside, but available

What is this I have in my hand, boys and girls? A flashlight! What do you do with it? Shine it in the dark! Turn this on for me. It doesn't work! What could be wrong? Let's look inside. Oops! There are no batteries!

The flashlight is no good without the batteries to give it power. We are somewhat like that. Without Jesus in our hearts we really cannot do any of the good things we know we should. If Jesus is not in our lives, we cannot love and share his joy with others.

When you put the batteries in the flashlight, it works. When we have Jesus in us, our light can also shine so that all will see his power in us.

Tonight in the sermon we are going to talk about how Jesus being in us can help us control our anger and bad feelings.

Lent 5

Angry Hands

The Prelude

The Opening Hymn *(Suggestions)*
"When I Survey the Wondrous Cross"

The Invocation
Leader: We come this day to worship and praise our God of love;
People: God the Father, Son and Holy Spirit. Amen

The Old Testament Lesson   Deuteronomy 19:15-21

The Psalm

Psalm 27 (Paraphrased)

Leader: The Lord is my light and my salvation, who can frighten me?
People: He is the strength of my life, of what can I be afraid?
Men: When my enemies attacked me, telling lies about me, they were not successful.
Women: Even though I seem to be surrounded by people who wish me evil I will be confident in the Lord.
People: In times of trouble he shields me from danger;
In days of evil he covers me with his love.
Leader: I am confident that you will always stand with me and protect me.
Men: When closest friends or even family desert me you stick with me.
Women: You cannot forsake me!
All: Show me the way for my life, O Lord.
Leader: Protect me from those that would wish me harm.
People: It feels sometimes like liars are coming at me from all sides; trying to hurt me.
Leader: I know that I shall see God's goodness, even here in the land of the living!
All: Be patient and wait on the Lord.
He will provide strength and courage.
Wait, I say, on the Lord!

62

The New Testament Lesson   Matthew 26:57-68

Anthem

The Children's Message

The Sermon Hymn *(Suggestions)*
   "Come to Calvary's Holy Mountain"
   "Cast Thy Burden upon the Lord"

The Sermon *Angry Hands*   Psalm 26:5-6

The Hymn of Response *(Suggestions)*
   "A Lamb Goes Uncomplaining Forth"
   "I Will Sing of My Redeemer"

The Offering

Anthem

The Prayers

The Benediction
   Pastor: Now may the God of all grace be with you;
            May he shield you with his powerful right hand,
            May his everlasting arms enfold you,
            May he smile upon you,
            And touch you with his peace.
   People: Amen

The Closing Hymn *(Suggestions)*
   "Now the Light Has Gone Away"
   "God Be with You Till We Meet Again"

The Postlude

Lent 6
Estranged Hands

Text: *Psalm 143:5-7*

I remember the days of long ago; I meditate on all your works and consider what your hands have done. I spread out my hands to you; my soul thirsts for you like a parched land. Answer me quickly, O Lord; my spirit faints with longing. Do not hide your face from me or I will be like those who go down to the pit.

Textual Comments:

David authors this penitential Psalm. In v. 2, he states plainly that one cannot stand before God in judgment and expect vindication on the basis of his merits.

v. 6   The writer's recognition of his own spiritual need and a brief meditative review (v. 5) of God's mighty acts inspire this prayer for a renewed relationship.

v. 7   *Answer me quickly* is the Psalmist's request. Do not remove yourself from me or I will be lost, is his concern.

Sermon Outline: *Estranged Hands*

Introduction: Broken relationships between an individual and God are frequently due to unresolved guilt.

I. *Our own feeble effort to remove guilt's traces from our own hands is never adequate.*
   A. Guilt, until it is resolved, can put barriers between us and God.
   B. Guilt can interrupt earthly relationships.
   C. Guilt can only be resolved through the merits of Jesus Christ.

II. *Christ comes with an invitation away from guilt and into a forgiven, sealed relationship with him.*
   A. The Psalmist's prayer offers for you and me the proper approach.
      1. "My soul thirsts for you." This admission of need is the proper beginning.

    2. "Consider what your hands have done." A review of God's gracious activities for us in Christ reassures us of his forgiveness.

    3. "Do not hide your face from me." The faith statement that apart from him we are nothing, is the ongoing attitude that should be seen in the penitent.

  B. Jesus comes as the fulfilment of the Psalmist's need and of ours. In him there is forgiveness and restoration.

Conclusion:

Christ resolves our guilt and draws us to himself by grace through faith.

Estranged Hands

Text: Psalm 143:5-7

Introduction:

In the early spring and late fall of each year, the Ladies Aid of our congregation has a rummage sale. Shortly after the last sale, I received the following note, enclosed in a package with a small trinket. The writer says, "I write this to my shame. You may feel this is nothing, but to me I've made myself lower than Judas who received thirty pieces of silver for his soul. I must make this right to please my Lord. One sin is as great as another, none is big or small, all is sin. To explain: I was at your Rummage Sale and carried a bag to put things in I planned to buy. The trinket you find was in the bag as I walked to the counter. I knew it was there, but the lady overlooked it and I was guilty of not telling her. Therefore, I was not charged for it. I felt it was so small she may have even given it to me. But this is no reason to be dishonest and grieve my Lord. Please forgive me. You may not believe it, but this small thing has cut off my fellowship in prayer with my Lord. And I believe he will forgive me when I make it right. I don't know what else to say except, I'm sorry."

I

*Our own feeble efforts to remove guilt traces
from our hands are never adequate*

Obviously this person was terribly burdened. The weight of her sin interrupted her spiritual relationship with the Lord. Guilt can do that because it reminds us of how unholy we are and how fragmented our relationships are with God and with others. Like a child who knows he has done wrong and is afraid to face his parents, even though they may be unaware of his error, so we, too, recognizing that we are sinners, find guilt to be a barrier between us and our God.

I feel certain that the person who wrote this note had gone through many days of anguish, feelings of loneliness and rejection. You can sense it in her wavering penmanship as she said, "This small thing has cut off my fellowship with my Lord." What a terrible burden!

All the efforts of humankind cannot excuse such guilt. You can see in this brief note that the person writing it admits she tried to rationalize. "It's a small item. No one will miss it. It doesn't cost much. It's worth very little. I've paid enough for the other things." The individual probably also tried to excuse it by saying, "Well, they made plenty of money. I'm poor, I'm in more need of this than they are." As obvious as the person's efforts are at explaining away her sin, just as obvious is the fact that it did not work. She could not find peace or resolve for her guilt in such excuses. Her rationalizations only caused the guilt to worsen.

Added to the burden of guilt and the brokenness of this individual's relationship with God, I'm also certain that her human nature caused her to wonder if maybe the people who accompanied her to the sale, or others around her, knew of her sin. Her guilt caused her to feel alienated or separated from the others. Guilt builds barriers between individuals and God. It also builds barriers between people.

Guilt is a scar. It's a reminder of sin. Across the back of my hand is a long scar. It reminds me of an accident caused by the foolishness of my efforts at repairing a garage door. Every time I look at my hand, I am reminded of how inept I really am. Guilt is a scar. It is a reminder that we are sinners. Guilt is a reminder of the scars that exist on our heart. It gives testimony to the many times we have transgressed God's will. Our guilt scars remind us that God would have a perfect right to break his relationship with us.

The scar on my hand is healed. It serves as a reminder, but it no longer interrupts the function of my hand. While I do not forget the error, the ability of my hand to be used is as great as it ever was. It has been restored. In Jesus Christ, we are extended the invitation to give him our guilt as we confess our wrong and find in him the peace of forgiveness and the restoration of our relationship with the Father. From the Cross of Calvary, Jesus cries out, "Father, forgive them." It is his plea as he pays the price to make that plea effective, that the God of our creation would set aside our guilt and declare us innocent through the merits of God's own Son, Jesus.

Our guilt is real, for we have truly sinned. There is no denying that the woman stole from the Rummage Sale. The scar on my hand is from an accident that really happened. That is the exact reason why God truly came in the person of his Son — to resolve the matter of sin in humankind, to pay the price and restore God's people to a relationship with him.

God doesn't just forget about sin. He resolves it in Jesus Christ. He doesn't just say to you and me, "Oh, remember them no more," but he tells us that indeed our sin works against our relationship with him. But he's resolved our sin in Jesus Christ by paying for the wrong in the righteousness of his own son.

II
Christ comes with an invitation away from sin and into a forgiven, sealed relationship with him

The Psalmist's prayer offers for you and me what would be a good approach as we are concerned to deal with our guilt in a healthy manner, and to acknowledge our God's loving forgiveness and restoration of us. First, the Psalmist says (verse 6): "My soul thirsts for you." It is his admission of need. That is the proper beginning place for each of us. We must acknowledge that we have guilt, that it is real, that it is true, that we are in need. Our spirits thirst for the Lord, for his forgiveness, and with that forgiveness the reaffirmation of our fellowship with him.

Secondly, the Psalmist says (verse 5): "I meditate on all your works and consider what your hands have done." If we, together with King David the writer, take but just a few moments and meditate briefly on the gracious activities of our God, we can find great comfort and reassurance even in the face of guilt. God gave up his own Son. Will he fail now to forgive and restore us as his people? The price has been paid. What more needs to be done than for us to accept this gracious gift of our Lord? When we consider all the history of God's grace as it relates to us individually and personally, we must feel affirmed. Through the waters of our Baptism, God has attached us to the history of his grace. The testimony of his grace reassures us that God's forgiveness is ours.

Thirdly, the Psalmist says (verse 7): "Do not hide your face from me." From deep within our heart our faith should continually plead that God would be near to us. He has given us Word and Sacrament as a means of being held near to him. It should always be our concern that we would walk close to the Lord, for only then can we put aside sin. Only through a faith relationship with our God can we overcome the burdens of our guilt and see the positive aspects of our relationship with him.

The Psalmist prayed that God would look favorably upon him

in the midst of his struggle with guilt and sin. God heard his prayer in the person of Jesus Christ, for he is the fulfilment of all of the prayers of those who preceeded him and he is the fulfilment of the prayers of each of us, that God, seeing us burdened by our sin, would wipe away the guilt that is ours and restore us once again into that relationship with him. Jesus Christ came to do that. He made it effective in each of us as he has called us by name and claimed us as his own. The message of the Cross is that our guilt is resolved in Jesus Christ. In his hands are our freedom, forgiveness and salvation.

May we hear the invitation of our Savior, even as the hymnist wrote: "Come, O sinners, one and all, come accept his invitation. Come, obey his gracious call, come and take his free salvation. Firmly in these words believe: Jesus sinners will receive." We are not God's estranged people. We are his forgiven children.

Children's Message

Object: two children
(best to prepare them before hand)

I am going to have [John and Mary] help me act out a little scene. Pretend I am the teacher at school. I have found John and Mary fighting.

Teacher: John! Mary! Stop your fighting this instant!
Mary: But he pulled my hair.
John: And she slapped me in the face.
Teacher: Neither complaint is cause for fighting. We should want to be friends, not enemies. Now, each of you tell the other one you're sorry.
John: I'm sorry.
Mary: I'm sorry.
Teacher: Shake hands now and make up.
Children: *(shake hands)*

Have you seen things like that happen before? How sad it would have been if John and Mary would have stayed angry and not played with each other or spoken to each other. That would have been wrong.

It is not good for us to hold bad feelings that separate us from each other. It is even worse when we have bad feelings in us that keep us away from Jesus and his love. Jesus forgives all the wrongs we do. He wants each of us to know that we can come to him and be sure that he will receive us as his friend.

Tonight's sermon will talk about Jesus' forgiveness and how he wants us to be close to him.

Lent 6

Estranged Hands

The Prelude

The Opening Hymn *(Suggestions)*
"O Dearest Jesus"
"Calvary Covers It All"
"O the Deep, Deep Love of Jesus"

The Invocation

The Old Testament Lesson   Deuteronomy 21:1-9

The New Testament Lesson   Matthew 27:11-26

The Conversation
Leader: "When Pilate saw that his talk was of no use, but that a riot was liable to break out, he took water and washed his hands before the crowd, saying:

Pilate: "I am innocent of the blood of this just man. But do as you wish."

Men: Did you hear that? He thinks a little water and he's off the hook.

Pilate: Now wait a minute. You're not going to accuse me of condemning an innocent man to death.

Women: So, you admit he's innocent?

Pilate: Well, he certainly hasn't done anything legally wrong by the government standards. His worst crime is that he offended the Jewish church leaders.

People: But you're still allowing him to be put to death?

Pilate: What choice do I have? The mob — they're liable to riot and cause a lot of vandalism and uproar. If news of that ever got back to my superiors. . .

Men: So a little water and elbow-grease and you're innocent!

Pilate: O, come on. You make me sound so bad. Well, it's no worse than some of the things that you do.

People: Such as?

Pilate: When you break your Mom's favorite plate, and then when she asks you who did it you say your brother or sister did. Or the situation where you know that you have offended someone, but instead of going to that person and asking forgiveness, you come to church and say a general confession and think that that takes care of the relationship.

People: I see what you mean.

Women: It's pretty easy to just hope that those sins will go away;

Men: That everyone will just forget about them.

Leader: Guilt can't be just washed away in water, or left till we hope it is forgotten. The only solvent for guilt is the blood of Jesus. That very blood that was shed because of Pilate's refusal to stand up for what is right, and our own tendency for doing likewise. Together let us wash our guilty hands in his blood, that cleanses us from every spot and stain.

All: We come, Lord, with our guilty hands, to you. Wash us, clean us. In your holy name. Amen

Anthem

The Children's Message

The Sermon Hymn *(Suggestions)*
    "My Song Is Love Unknown"
    "O Sacred Head, Now Wounded"
    "Amazing Grace"

The Sermon *Estranged Hands*   Psalm 143:5-7

The Hymn of Response *(Suggestions)*
    "Not All the Blood of Beasts"
    "Jesus Loves Me"
    "Children of the Heavenly Father"

The Offering

Anthem

The Prayers

The Benediction

Leader: Now may the God of all grace go with you;
May he look down in love and favor upon you
and guide you on your homeward way;
May he enfold you in his arms,
and grant you his peace throughout this night.

All: Amen

The Closing Hymn *(Suggestions)*

"Sweet the Moments, Rich In Blessing"
"Jesus Paid It All"
"God, Who Made the Earth and Heaven"

The Postlude

Maundy Thursday
Serving Hands

Text: *Psalm 92:4-5*

For you make me glad by your deeds, O Lord; I sing for joy at the works of your hands. How great are your works, O Lord, how profound your thoughts!

Textual Comments:

It is good to praise the Lord. The opening words of the Psalm reflect well its overall theme. The Psalmist offers praise for the many instances when the Lord has blessed the people through his deeds.

> v. 4   *The works of your hand* — the joy to be offered is in response to the redemptive actions of God.

> v. 5   The Lord has done great things; his actions proceed from his kind and loving thoughts.

Sermon Outline: *Serving Hands*

Introduction: Being a servant to others is not an agreeable role to most of us.

I. *Jesus comes as "the work of the Lord's hands" to serve our needs.*
   A. As the guest of Jesus, we are invited to this special meal which he has prepared with us in mind.
   B. The humble nature of Jesus' service can be observed as he washes the feet of the disciples on the first Maundy Thursday.
   C. Today we are still recipients of his service. He offers a meal in which he is the host and the substance.

II. *Our joyous response to the Lord's service should be in full recognition of all that we receive.*
   A. As guests, we come to the meal humble and appreciative for what we are about to receive.
   B. Being guests at such a holy meal, we receive the gift in the faith that our Lord is truly sharing himself with us.
   C. Knowing the goodness of our Lord, we receive the meal in the certainty that through this means we are blessed.

Conclusion:

The meal offered to us is served by the Lord's hand. He is our host. His hand is extended in invitation. Come, all is ready.

Serving Hands

Text: Psalm 92:4-5

Introduction:

Being a servant to others is not a role that is generally sought after in our society today. We tend to be a people who seek to be served, rather than offering to serve. However, Jesus said of himself that he came to serve, not to be served. He elevated for us the servant's position as he said to us, "Whoever wants to become great among you must be your servant." The entire message of salvation can be summed up by saying, "Jesus came to serve us in our needs." That is no more clearly seen than in these final days of his earthly ministry. The passion of Holy Week paints the picture of Jesus as a suffering servant. He came to serve and he continues to serve you and me in special ways.

I

Jesus comes as "the work of the Lord's hands"
to serve our needs

This is Maundy Thursday, the day on which we recognize and celebrate that Jesus, as part of his service to us, instituted the special meal of his own body and blood, the meal which was prepared with you and me in mind. By the Gospel and the faith that's been worked in our hearts, we are invited as Jesus' guests to this special meal. Like the twelve who sat together with him that first night, we have been called into discipleship. We have been invited spiritually to the upper room to partake in this most special meal, to fellowship with our Lord and one another, to sing hymns, to share the Word, and to break this most holy bread together. Jesus is our host. He invites us as his guest in order that he, out of his loving hand, might serve you and me.

If there would be any doubt about Jesus' intent to serve, it is dispelled as he performs the most humble of acts. The Apostle John tells us, "Jesus proceeded to wash the feet of his disciples." What a menial task! And yet, it is the Lord's intent to communicate to the twelve and to you and me, as modern disciples, that he comes to serve — to serve *our* needs, not his own. He puts himself in position to accomplish our cleansing, something that we could not do for ourselves. He comes to serve that we might see his all-surpassing love, and in response might strive to love him and one another in a similar way. Let there be no doubt that this is the God of all creation. This is he who takes upon himself flesh, in order to become the suffering servant of humankind, that in his service the needs of all humanity might be met. The required forgiveness, life, and salvation could be obtained in him alone as he humbles himself and provides that service which no other human could offer, the service of working our salvation.

Maybe you are one who says, "How thrilling it would have been to have participated in that upper room two thousand years ago, to be a participant in this special meal and foot washing!" How thankful we may be that we are able to be there in faith. However, do not doubt that we are still recipients of the Lord's service, and are participants in all that he offers. The worth, the care, the concern of all the actions that occurred then, are still offered to you and me today as the Lord has given this holy meal to us and perpetuates its value and effectiveness to us through his Word. We are recipients of that special meal as the Lord, through his word, takes the simple means of bread and wine and gives to us the holy substance of his body and blood for the forgiveness of our sins, the strengthening of our faith. The meal is offered to resassure us that we are the guests of the very Son of God, our Savior and Lord. He offers to us a meal in which he is both the host and at the same time the substance we receive. For as he has gathered us around his table, he says, "Take and eat, this is my body; take and drink, this is my blood." He is himself the priest who offers the sacrifice and he is also the sacrificial lamb that is offered, of which you and I become partakers. This is one of the great deeds of which the Psalmist speaks, the deeds that make you and me glad. Jesus Christ comes to serve our needs out of his compassion for us as his people.

II
Our joyous response to the Lord's service
should be in full recognition of all that we receive

Honored guests — that's what we are! How else can we consider ourselves, for certainly we have not deserved or earned the invitation to this meal. We have been invited out of the mercy of our Lord.

Having received such a blessed invitation, how, then, should we come? Obviously, if you or I received an invitation to some function which we felt was far above our status in life, possibly some small intimate reception at the White House, or some other such activity, I can well imagine that we would arrive there very humble and appreciative for the opportunity of participating in such an event. Really, our attitude in coming to the Lord's meal should be no different. We should come in all humility, in full awareness that we have too frequently been involved in those things that would make us unclean and ill prepared to participate in this holy meal. Yet, here we are as the Master's guest. The servant who lives in the gloom and darkness of the pig pen has been invited to the Master's table. The Master becomes the servant as he offers the most precious of meals. Surely, we would have to be humbled as we come to the Lord's table, for we are sinners invited into the presence of our God.

With humility we also offer our thanks for such a gift. We, through the ministry of our church, assist people in obtaining groceries when they are unable to provide for themselves. Almost always the people are grateful and thankful for what they have received, for they realize that their lives could not be sustained apart from having sustenance for their bodies. The meal to which the Lord invites you and me, this meal of his own body and blood, is offered to sustain our spirit, to give us the strength that is needed to reaffirm our relationship with him and to give us the certainty of our tomorrows in his kingdom. The Lord offers this meal. Our proper attitude and response should be one of thanksgiving, recognizing that we have not earned it, but that the meal has been given by the grace of God. We in thanksgiving say, "Lord, thank you for all that you give. Your great and wonderful deeds make me glad."

Faith, too, is an aspect of worthy reception as we come to the Lord's meal. He says, "Sit, eat, be a guest at my table; this is my body, this is my blood given for you." What he says is true. God created the world by the speaking of a word — "Let there be" — and there was. That same God shares himself with us through his Son's body and blood as he says, "Take and eat, this is my body." It is, in fact, what Jesus says it is, his own body and blood. But for it to benefit you and me in our lives, for us to receive the full blessing that the Lord intends through this meal, we must receive it believing. Through the eyes of faith we perceive that Jesus Christ has served us in sharing with you and me himself. In matters that go beyond human understanding or reason, the Lord imparts to us this special communion of earthly elements with the divine person of Jesus Christ. He shares with us the communion that exists between us and him as we gather at his table. He allows us in faith to commune with one another as we are bound as brothers and sisters through our participation in this one body and blood. Apart from faith, we deny the value of this meal for ourselves. It is in faith, the faith that the Spirit works in you and me, that we lay claim to the meal and the worth of that meal that the Lord puts before us.

A host invites his guest to the table in order that he or she can eat, be filled, and depart satisified, sustained to continue their living. God as our host is no different. He invites us to his table that in receiving this special meal we might be blessed, and that being so blessed we might be better prepared to live our lives to his glory.

Undoubtedly the most famous painting of the "Last Supper" is that one painted by Leonardo daVinci. He produced the picture in a setting that would have been familiar to the people of his time. It was an Italian dining room with an Italian table setting, with Jesus and the disciples placed around an Italian table. Artistic interpretation would suggest that daVinci believed that it was a meal offered for his time. You and I could have the same understanding today. The Lord extends his hand of service to you and me today. Jesus Christ is our host. Our Lord extends to you and me his invitation. "Come, all is ready."

Maundy Thursday

Serving Hands

The Invocation
Leader: It is with great joy we come into this house of worship to praise the name of God the Father,
People: whose love for us caused him to give up his son;
Leader: God the son,
People: whose service to us meant giving up his life;
Leader: and God the Holy Spirit,
People: whose work opens our hearts to his Word.
All: Amen

The Confession
Pastor: We kneel to confess our sins to our gracious heavenly Father.
All: Lord, you have placed me here in my family, school or place of work to serve others for you. You have even given me the ultimate model of serving, that of your son, who gave his life in service to me. Yet I have often failed to do your work. Through my words and actions I have rather tried to lord it over those around me. I think myself better than others of your children, and put them down to make myself feel good.
Forgive me, Lord, for these sins.
Pardon me for the times I have failed to recognize situations where I could be of service to you. Continue to use me, and put me in places where I can serve you.
Pastor: God has heard your prayer. Even before you asked he sent his forgiveness in the death of his son for you. Go now, forgiven, redeemed, and empowered to serve.
People: Amen

The Prelude

The Opening Hymn *(Suggestions)*
"Soul, Adorn Yourself with Gladness"
"O Jesus, I Have Promised"

The Salutation
Pastor: The Lord be with you.
People: And also with you.
Pastor: Let us pray. Lord, as on that first Maundy Thursday you took a towel and washed the feet of your disciples, fill us with your Spirit that we may serve one another. Through Jesus Christ, your son, our Lord, who lives and reigns with you and the Holy Spirit, one God, eternal.
People: Amen

The Old Testament Lesson   Jeremiah 31:31-34
(After the reading:)
Pastor: This is the word of the Lord.
People: Thanks be to God.

The New Testament Lesson   Hebrews 10:15-39
(same response)

Anthem

The Holy Gospel   Luke 22:7-20
(Before the reading:)
Pastor: The Holy Gospel according to Saint Luke, the twenty second chapter, the seventh verse.
People: Glory be to you, O Lord.

(After the reading:)
Pastor: This is the Good News of our Lord.
People: Praise be to you, O Lord.

The Sermon Hymn *(Suggestions)*
    "The Death of Jesus Christ, Our Lord"
    "O Master, Let Me Walk with Thee"
    "We Are the Reason"

The Sermon *Serving Hands*   Psalm 92:4-5

The Hymn of Response *(Suggestions)*
    "When I Survey the Wondrous Cross"
    "In Remembrance"

The Offering

The Prayers

The Holy Communion

The Consecration

The Pax
> Pastor: The peace of the Lord be with you always.
> People: And also with you.

> *The Canticle (Suggestions)*
> "Draw Near and Take the Body of the Lord"
> "Let Us Break Bread Together On Our Knees"

The Thanksgiving
> Pastor: Oh, give thanks to the Lord, for he is good.
> People: And his mercy endures forever.

The Benediction
> Pastor: As you have been served by our Lord Jesus Christ, go
> forth now and serve those whom the Lord has placed
> around you, and the blessing of our God, the Father,
> Son and Holy Spirit, be with you.
> People: Amen

The Closing Hymn *(Suggestions)*
> "Sent Forth by God's Blessing"
> "Savior, Thy Dying Love"

The Postlude

Good Friday
Pierced Hands

Text: *Psalm 22:14-18*

I am poured out like water, and all my bones are out of joint. My heart has turned to wax; it has melted away within me. My strength is dried up like a potsherd, and my tongue sticks to the roof of my mouth; you lay me in the dust of death. Dogs have surrounded me; a band of evil men has encircled me, they have pierced my hands and my feet. I can count all my bones; people stare and gloat over me. They divide my garments among them and cast lots for my clothing.

Textual Comments:

This is a prophetic Psalm that vividly describes the passions of the Lord. Jesus himself quotes the opening verse from the Cross, "My God, my God, why have you forsaken me?"

v. 14   The Psalmist depicts one who is in tremendous physical agony and is incapable of doing anything about his own condition.

v. 15   There is little strength left in the one suffering. He is near death.

v. 16   Suffering as he is, he is disgusted by the evil people who surround him. "They have pierced my hands and my feet," is an obvious reference to crucifixion.

v. 17   The body is wasting, but the onlookers, the gawkers still gather around.

v. 18   The dividing of the sufferer's garments is but one more insult. They take his only possession.

Sermon Outline: *Pierced Hands*

Introduction: Jesus' hands are pierced in his crucifixion.

I. Jesus' crucifixion was God's great sacrifice for humankind.
  A. Crucifixion was the cruelest of punishments.
    1. Only the worst criminals were sent to the cross.
    2. In the case of Jesus, it was an unjust crucifixion.
  B. Jesus was crucified in our stead.
    1. He went to the Cross with our guilt on his hands.
    2. The nails that pierced his hand were rightly meant for us.

II. Jesus' crucifixion destroyed the guilt that should condemn each of us.
  A. Jesus was crucified on what we have entitled "Good Friday."
    1. Why should such a day be called good?
    2. Our guilt was crucified in the body of Christ. (Isaiah 53)
    3. Sins nailed to the Cross are sins removed forever. (Psalm 103:12)
  B. May the nail-pierced hands of Jesus be for you the symbol of your eternal forgiveness.

Conclusion:
  Christ died for you! His hands were pierced for you, your forgiveness and your salvation.

Pierced Hands

Text: Psalm 22:14-18

Introduction:

It is amazing, when we read Psalm 22, to realize that it was written a thousand years before Jesus was born. Yet, King David, the Psalm's author, speaks in the most descriptive terms of the coming Messiah's suffering.

I
Jesus' hands were pierced
in his crucifixion

Crucifixion, of all the punishments ever devised, must be the most gruesome of all. When one was crucified his body was laid across the limbs of a cross, and through his hands and his feet were placed large nails. Then the cross was uprighted so that the body hung in mid air, the weight of the body pulling on the wounds. Literally, the body became disjointed and began to cave in. The lungs would be crushed as the rib cage collapsed. The heart would finally give out from all of the pressure that was placed upon it. It was a gruesome and horrible death, one that took hours and sometimes days.

What an unjust punishment! We probably would not tolerate such cruelty in our society. We debate today whether capital punishment is even right or proper in a civilized world. We would never support such a horrendous and horrible form of punishment as crucifixion. Never! Even in the day of Jesus, one could not crucify a Roman citizen. It was only the people who did not hold citizenship who could be crucified; and of those people, this punishment was reserved for the very worst. Crucifixion was inflicted only on the most hardened criminals.

Why, then, was this man, Jesus of Nazareth, led to the hill to be crucified? Why? What had he done? What crime had he committed that they would stand him up and accuse him of such dastardly deeds? Why would they take his life? What crime had he committed that his own countrymen would call out, "Crucify him, crucify him?" What could cause such anger and hate?

Jesus' crucifixion was an unjust punishment. Even Pontius Pilate, the Governor and judge, said, "I can find no reason in this man that we should crucify him. I cannot come in my own conscience to the conclusion that we ought to take this man's life away from him. I'll beat him to satisfy you. I'll mock him to satisfy you. But I cannot murder him for you." But the crowd cried all the more, "Crucify him, crucify him!" They wanted his blood, his life. Why? Was there any just reason? Of all the crimes that humanity has done against other humans, the crucifixion of Jesus had to be the most unjust of all, for there was no sin in this man; there was no wrong; there was no anger. There was no hate in him. This was the sinless, perfect Son of God.

Jesus was the very Son of God who just days before had raised Lazarus from the dead. This was God's Son who had been welcomed by the city of Jerusalem with shouts of "Hosanna, blessed is he who comes in the name of the Lord!"

He comes in the name of the Lord, and they're going to crucify him? How just can that be? Yet, it was the unjust nature of that crucifixion that brings you and me to stand at the foot of the Cross today, to see the Lord. While it was so unjust, you and I recognize that he was guilty. He was put on the Cross with guilt on his hands. It is not *his* guilt — that is what makes it unjust. He went to the Cross with sin-covered hands. He went to the Cross with soiled hands, but he had not done the wrong. He went to the Cross bearing the guilt, the scars, all the wrongs of you and me. It was unjust that he should go and be laid on that Cross, because he was being put there for things that he had not done. He was being put there for the things that you and I have done and will do in our lives.

There was guilt on his hands. It was the guilt of the world. When the nails pierced his hands and the blood gushed forth, when the flesh was separated by the coarse metal that inflicted such pain, you and I know that the nails that pierced him were really intended for us. They were intended for us, because the guilt was borne on those hands, the guilt that the nail intended to pierce and to punish, was not the guilt of the One being nailed to the Cross, but it was our guilt. The guilt that needed to be nailed to that tree was not the guilt of the innocent Son of God, but it was the guilt of God's people who had rebelled against God and turned away from him in their thoughts, actions and words. The guilt that was there was not his. The punishment that was dealt out against that guilt was pain that he did not deserve. All the pain had been rightfully earned by you and me and our brothers and sisters in this world.

The nails were put through the flesh to punish the guilt, but it was not his guilt, it was ours. It was *our* guilt that was crucified on that tree. It was our guilt that was nailed to the tree on that day in the person of God's Son. Satisfaction was necessary before God if we were to be brought into a relationship with God. God's wrath and God's anger against sin had to be satisfied. God doesn't just excuse sin. God doesn't just say, "Oh, forget about it, it's all right." God says, "No, that is sin, and sin must be dealt with." Sin must be eradicated. Sin and the death that it causes has a price that must be paid. It was paid on that Good Friday when nails pierced his hand. Jesus was the payment. He was the only adequate and sufficient payment.

Our guilt, our sin, our wrong was laid on that tree in the hands of Jesus Christ. When he went so willingly to the Cross, bearing that timber on his own shoulders and carrying it to Golgotha, he was carrying not only the weight of the lumber that made up the Cross, but also the weight of the sins of each one of us. He was carrying us to the hill that there we might be crucified with him, in order that on Easter morn we might also be resurrected with him.

Isaiah the prophet says, "He was pierced for our transgression, he was crushed for our iniquities; the punishment that brought us peace was upon him, and by his wounds we are healed."

I remember as a child wondering why in the world they call today "Good"! Not long ago I was at chapel with our Kindergarten students. I asked, "Why do you think they call it Good Friday?" A little toothless fellow right in front of me, one who could hardly speak in a clear tone, said, "Well, they call it Good Friday because Jesus died because he loves me." It's the truth! That's what makes it good: all the agony of the Cross, all the pain and suffering, all the agony that can be seen visited upon this man who didn't deserve it. It is good because it was done for you and me. It is good, because it is by this price of his hands being nailed to the tree that your guilt and my guilt have been set aside and crucified with him. In him you have life. As we die with him on this day, it is certain, Saint Paul says, that knowing him in faith we will be resurrected with him on the day that is to come. It is our sin that causes him to be nailed to the tree. It is almost as if you and I were wielding the hammer that sends the spikes through the flesh. Every sin is one more blow that puts the nails through his hands. He willingly receives each blow. He does not cry out, "Father, why are you doing this injustice to me?'' He doesn't cry out, ''Father, they don't deserve this!'' But he rather cries out, ''Father, forgive them.'' And the Father *does* forgive you and me. The nail that pierces his hand is the nail sent through him for you and me.

The Psalmist will write later (Psalm 103) that because the Messiah is offered up, God looks at us in a different way. He says, ''As far as the east is from the west, so far has he removed our transgressions from us.'' In other words, they exist no longer in the mind of God. God does not see the Cross where our sins exist. He rather sees living people alive in his Son, Jesus Christ. Our sins are nailed to the Cross in the hands of Jesus Christ. Our wrongs are lost in his blood. They are no longer visible to God and can no longer be counted against you and me. They are nailed to a Cross that is forgotten in God's mind, a symbol of death that is transformed into the great statement of life, our life now and eternally. Unnecessarily we live with guilt in our lives. Many of us walk around day after day bearing burdens that are no longer ours. They have been nailed to the Cross of Jesus Christ.

Today I would like to give you a gift. After the offering is received, the ushers are going to pass among you a box of nails. The nails have been painted in a way to remind you that the blood that was poured out on the cross of Jesus Christ is for you. That nail is a gift, a Good Friday gift. It is a gift to remind you that by the nail that pierced the hand of Jesus Christ, God put away your sin and your guilt forever. Put it in your pocket. Remember the nail that pierced the hand of Jesus Christ was a nail that was deserved by you and me, but received by him, so that you and I could know life.

Good Friday — A Noonday Service

Pierced Hands

The Prelude

The Opening Hymn *(Suggestions)*
"O Perfect Life of Love"
"In the Cross of Christ I Glory"
"Were You There?"

The Invocation
Leader: On this most holy day we come to this place to behold our God —
People: God the Father, God the Son, and God the Holy Spirit. Amen

The Collect
Leader: *Let us pray:* Almighty God, whose love divine caused you to spend your life for us, we thank you that those pierced and bleeding hands reach out in love to us. Hold us firmly as your own until we come into your glory, in the name of our Savior, Jesus Christ.
People: Amen

The Old Testament Lesson   Isaiah 52:13—53:12

Those Hands *[**Hammer strikes]*
**
Leader: Look at them! Is it possible? Can they be the same hands?
People: The same hands that blessed children?
Men: The same hands that comforted sinners?
Women: The same hands that healed the blind?
People: The same hands that broke the bread?
**
Leader: Yet now I see them outstretched and pierced; writhing from pain
People: the life-blood steadily dripping from them;
All: For me! Those hands are pierced for me!

Voice: My God, my God, why hast thou forsaken me? *(Psalm 22:1)*

Leader: Yet we esteemed him stricken, smitten of God and afflicted. (Isaiah 53:4b)

People: He was despised and rejected by men; a man of sorrows and acquainted with grief. (Isaiah 53:3)

Leader: All who see me laugh at me. They make faces at me and shake their heads. (Psalm 22:7)

People: He trusted in God, let him deliver him, if he delights in him. (Psalm 22:8)

Voice: Father, forgive them, for they know not what they do.

Leader: Mocked, despised, rejected, suspended between heaven and hell, those same hands are outstretched in forgiveness.

People: Lord, forgive me. Those hands are pierced for me!

Voice: It is finished.

Leader: All the Father sent him to do;

Men: to be born in humility,

Women: to suffer the torture of a criminal;

People: to die in loneliness.

Leader: All was now complete.

People: God's own sacrifice of himself was complete. Finished.

Leader: Those pierced hands hang limp and cold;

People: the warm life-blood now drained from the veins, cleansing all on whom it falls.

Leader: Those hands were pierced by me.

People: Those hands were pierced for me!

Voice: And God saw everything he had done, and behold it was very good. *(Genesis 1:31)*

Anthem

The Holy Gospel John 19:17-30

The Sermon Hymn *(Suggestions)*
"Jesus, All Your Labor Vast"
"Beneath the Cross of Jesus"
"There Is a Green Hill Far Away"

The Sermon *Pierced Hands*   Psalm 22:14-18

The Hymn of Response *(Suggestions)*
"Upon the Cross Extended"
"What Wondrous Love"
"Wounded for Me"

The Offering

Anthem

The Prayers

The Benediction
Leader: May our dear Lord bless you and keep you;
May his loving face shine upon you and be gracious to
you;
May those pierced hands ever enfold you;
And touch you with his peace.
People: Amen

The Closing Hymn *(Suggestion)*
"O Sacred Head, Now Wounded"

The Postlude

90

Good Friday Tenebrae

Into Thy Hands

The Processional Music
"The Royal Banners Forward Go"   V. H. Fortunatus

The Invocation

The Prayer

The Hymn "Jesus, I Will Ponder Now"

I Believe in Jesus Christ . . .
> The Scripture: Matthew 27:1-10
> The Hymn: "Jesus, Refuge of the Weary"

Who Suffered Under Pontius Pilate
> The Scripture: Matthew 27:11-26
> The Hymn:
>> "O Dearest Jesus, What Law Hast Thou Broken?"
> The Scripture: Matthew 27:27-31
> The Choir: "O Sacred Head, Now Wounded"

Was Crucified
> The Scripture: Matthew 27:32-44
> The Choir: "O Dearest Lord, Thy Sacred Head"
>   D. N. Johnson

. . . Died . . .
> The Scripture: Matthew 27:45-50
> The Hymn: "Stricken, Smitten, and Afflicted"
> The Scripture: Matthew 27:51-56
> The Choir: "Wondrous Love"   arr. P. Christiansen

And Was Buried.
> The Scripture: Matthew 27:57-66
> The Hymn: "O Darkest Woe"

The Prayers

Anthem "Lamb of God"   F. M. Christiansen

The Sealing of the Tomb

The Silent Departure

Easter
Living Hands

Text: *Psalm 118:15-17*
> *Shouts of joy and victory resound in the tents of the righteous: "The Lord's right hand is lifted high; the Lord's right hand has done mighty things!" I will not die but live, and will proclaim what the Lord has done.*

Textual Comments:
Luther considered this his favorite Psalm. It has a Messianic character closely related to the overall theme of praise and thanksgiving.

v. 15   Great joy exists among the households of Israel, because the Lord's "right hand," his omnipotent power, has done mighty things.

v. 17   Israel has been delivered from a life-and-death struggle. By God's right hand the people have been delivered to proclaim to all what the Lord has done.

Sermon Outline: *Living Hands*
Introduction: Christ is Risen! That is the good news of the mighty thing our Lord has done for you and me. Therefore, with the Psalms we can affirm, "I shall not die . . ." Christ is Alive! The Easter message is that we, too, are alive in him.

   I. Having been given life in Christ, we are to live in the full confidence of God's grace.
      A. We live in a time when many things might challenge our confidence as Christians.
      B. The resurrection of Jesus is God's mighty act that guarantees to us life in the fullest sense.

  II. Our living centers in our new life given by God's right hand, his son, Jesus Christ.
      A. New life in Christ is the root principle of the Christian faith.
        1. New life gives us a unique perspective on living.
        2. New life is given to us personally; it is worked in our Baptism, held through our faith, and made functional by grace in our living.
      B. New life in Christ grants a fortitude for life and in the face of death.

Conclusion:
"The Lord's Right Hand has done mighty things! I will not die, but live."

Living Hands

Text: Psalm 118:15-17

Introduction:

Christ is Risen! That is the good news of the mighty thing our Lord has done for you and me. Therefore, with the Psalmist we can affirm, "I shall not die." Christ is alive. The Easter message is that we, too, are alive in him. As Christians, we live in a time when many things might challenge our confidence in Christ. On this Easter morn we are full of joy and celebration, but there still looms around us that continuing struggle in the inner person. Recent experiences, personal or observed, might cause questions to rise in our mind as we see families breaking up, youth not holding to the values of their parents, illness and death coming when it seems so inappropriate. These and the many other challenges of our life might cause us to look at life rather skeptically, even as Christians.

I
Having been given life in Christ, we are to live in the full confidence of God's grace

The society in which we live seems to be in a time of flux. Many things are changing. Many values are not what they used to be. This, too, can cause us to look around and question, wonder, and doubt, regarding our life and our future. One might even wonder if God is still involved in our world and in our personal life. John Naisbitt, in a popular book entitled, *Megatrends*, says, "It is as though we have bracketed off the present from both the past and the future, for we are neither here nor there."[1] He capsulizes for us the feeling of many. We are at an in-between stage, a time of change. Do we approach that change with confidence or with fear?

The resurrection of Jesus Christ is God's answer to you and me regarding the changing, unstable condition of the world in which we live. There is no question that there is a great deal of change and challenge around us on every side. However, in the midst of it all stands the resurrected Christ. He has come as God's right hand into our world, to interject himself into our struggle, that we might have a living confidence in the God of our salvation — a sure confidence that nothing can overcome us nor destroy us.

Dietrich Bonhoeffer, the great German theologian martyred during the dictatorship of Adolf Hitler, speaking in his time of change and challenge said, "In that period inbetween the creation and the resurrection, we ward off madness with the perserving acts recalling His death, victory, and straining forward to what lies ahead."[2] God has done a mighty thing in resurrecting his Son from the dead. God sent his Son into the world to live on our behalf. He went to the Cross to die for our redemption. He stepped forth in resurrection to prove that all that he has done has been done well, and our salvation is complete in him.

Christ is Risen! His life, death, and resurrection are ours. Through him, united to him in faith, we live. In the fullest sense, we live both now and eternally. Lifted from the pit of human existence, contaminated as it is with death and the rule of Satan, we find new life, resurrection. This is our experience in God's grace through Christ Jesus. Our expectation for life should be high, having experienced God's love in such a magnificent way.

II
Our living centers in our new life
given by God's right hand, his Son, Jesus Christ

New life is the root principle of the Christian faith. We are no longer what we were. We are no longer attached to this world, its difficulties and problems. God's right hand has laid hold on us and lifted us above such struggles. Knowing the resurrected Christ, we cannot be drawn back into the depths of death and the struggles of earthly existence. New life has been given to each of us personally by God's grace. Through the waters of our Baptism we've been united into Jesus Christ. Saint Paul tells us that if we have union with him, we then have participation in his death and also in his resurrection. Today's celebration of the resurrection is a celebration not only of our Savior's rising, but also of the truth that we are resurrected together with him. By God's mercy we are united to Jesus Christ. God's Son came into the world to unite himself to us, to be our brother. By the miracle of God claiming us, sealing that claim in the waters of our Baptism, we have been united with the Savior so that we are recipients of his merits and worth, including his life.

We are participants in new life today through the faith that is ours. The faith that exists in your heart is testimony that God has been active in you. It is the thumb-print that gives proof that God has opened up your heart to receive the resurrected Christ, and in him to receive life. We are held in that faith so that Saint Paul can confidently say to the church at Rome, "There is nothing that can separate us from the love of God which is in Christ Jesus our Lord." God's right hand, his Son, Jesus Christ, has laid hold of you and me. Our faith is testimony to that truth.

Our new life in Jesus Christ is functional for you and me on a day to day basis. It provides for us a new perspective on life, a new power in our living, and a new ability to deal with the challenges, change, and struggles of our earthly walk. For every day God demonstrates his grace to us through the sharing of his word, through his body and blood as it is offered to us in the Sacrament of the Lord's Supper. God's grace is functional in our lives, giving testimony again and again of the new life that is ours and the price that was paid to make it all possible.

Knowing that we have been personally granted new life in Jesus Christ, our ability to look at our world and put it into a proper perspective should be greatly improved. I remember my grandfather telling a story regarding his neighbor on the farm. It seemed the neighbor was a man who complained a great deal about having to work in the soil and the dirt. He spoke of how menial a task farming was. "It lacked importance," he said. Finally, my grandfather became a little perturbed with the man's complaining. He said to him, "You're looking at this in totally the wrong way. You are a partner with God in growing beautiful plants and providing food for many people. You are a partner with the Creator of the world, taking a tiny seed, bringing it to full blossom and bloom for it to bear fruit to provide for the needs of other people. You're not a person who digs in the dirt, you're a partner with God in doing great and mighty things." These two men looked at the same task, with completely different perspectives. We as Christians live in the same world as all other people. Many do not hold the faith that you and I have by God's grace. Our faith is our claim to new life in Jesus Christ. Faith in the resurrected Christ gives us a new perspective. It is a perspective that allows us to live in the confidence of knowing that we are partners with our Lord Jesus Christ. We do not stand in this world alone, but we stand together with him. Whatever the change, whatever the challenge, in whatever in-between situation we find ourselves today, the Lord who promises us new life is there beside us. In him is new life and the certainty that life is eternal. We will not die.

The people in Tanzania, having this new perspective on life, have a unique custom in their Easter celebration. When they sing or shout "Hallelujah", they do it as a laugh. They go "Hallelujah, ha, ha, ha!" The custom states that they find such joy in the knowledge that Christ is risen, that they can laugh in the face of Satan and all the things of this world. What a great attitude of Christian confidence![3]

"The Lord's right hand has done mighty things. I will not die, but live." And live we should. Today, we should live as people who have seen the resurrected Christ with the certainty that in all of our tomorrows we will live with that same Christ in his everlasting kingdom. The church is always beautifully decorated on Easter morning. The bright colors and the beautiful decorations enhance our celebration. It is one of our traditions to make use of lilies as part of the decorations in our church. This morning I would like to suggest to you that there is possibly another plant that might be a more appropriate symbol for Easter. Perhaps we should consider the dandelion as our Easter flower. Granted, it is not as pretty as the lily, but its enduring quality speaks well of the Easter theme. I continually try and rid my lawn of dandelions and they repeatedly come back. I pull them up. I spray them with weed killer. But still they resurrect. I know of no other plant that can come through the cracks in my sidewalk or driveway. They pop their head through the concrete to prove their durability. No matter what you do to the dandelion, it seems to come back again and again. No persecution, no challenge, no struggle can seem to do away with the dandelion. The frailty of the Easter lily misses the truth of what we are as Christians. The frail petals and the temporary nature of the plant does not really describe what life we have in Christ. The dandelion may do it better, for there is no trial, there is no struggle, there is no challenge that can overcome us in God's grace. We have new life in Jesus Christ. God's right arm has done a mighty thing and we shall not die, but live.

May you live that life today in its fulness and tomorrow in

Christ's eternity. Christ is Risen! The Lord's right hand has done a mighty thing!

1. Naisbitt, John: *Megatrends*, Warner Books, N.Y., N.Y., 1982, pg. 249.
2. Quoted in "Parables, etc." Volume 4 No. 2, April 1984, Saratoga Press, Saratoga, Ca.
3. *Sermon Illustrations For the Gospel Lessons*, Concordia Publishing House, St. Louis, Mo., 1980, pg. 17.

Easter

Living Hands

The Prelude

The Processional Hymn *(Suggestion)*
"Jesus Christ Is Risen Today"

The Invocation
Pastor: We begin our celebration of victory in the name of the loving Father and of the living Son, and of the all-powerful Holy Spirit.
All: Amen

The Sentence for the Day
Pastor: Christ is risen!
People: He is risen indeed!
All: Alleluia! Alleluia!

The Kyrie
(Tune: Gelobt sei Gott)
O Lord, have mercy on us here.
O Christ, have mercy, our hearts cheer.
Have mercy on us, Lord, most dear.
Alleluia, Alleluia, Alleluia.

The Gloria in Excelsis
(Tune: "Lasst uns erfreuen)
Glory to God in highest heav'n.
And peace on earth, good will to men.
Alleluia, Alleluia.
We Praise, we bless, we worship you.
We glorify; give thanks to you
For your glory, power supernal,
Might, dominion, praise eternal, Alleluia!

Lord, Father, God, Almighty King,
Lord, Jesus Christ, to you we sing.

Alleluia, Alleluia.
And to the Spirit, Three in One,
Be glory now; the vict'ry won!
Christ has conquered, burst the prison;
Death is vanquished; he is risen! Alleluia!

The Salutation

Pastor: The Lord be with you.

People: And also with you.

Pastor: *Let us pray.* O Lord, on this day you rose triumphantly from the dead, showing that you had conquered sin and death. We thank you that your victory is now ours; that you have made peace with God on our behalf. Bless us now as we live in that victory. This we ask in the name of our living Savior, Jesus Christ.

All: Amen

The Old Testament Lesson   Exodus 15:1-11

The Epistle Lesson   1 Corinthians 15:1-11

Anthem

The Holy Gospel   Luke 24:1-11
or John 20:1-9 (10-18)

The Sermon Hymn *(Suggestions)*
"Awake, My Heart, with Gladness"
"Rejoice, the Lord Is King"

The Sermon *Living Hands*   Psalm 118:15-17

The Hymn of Response *(Suggestions)*
"At the Lamb's High Feast We Sing"
"Thine Is the Glory"
"Alleluia! Alleluia!"

The Offering

Anthem

The Prayers

(Without Communion)

The Benediction

The Recessional Hymn *(Suggestions)*
"I Know That My Redeemer Lives"
"Lift High the Cross"

The Postlude

(With Communion)

The Preparation
Pastor: It is appropriate as we come to the Lord's table that we should confess our sins.
All: Dear Lord, I come before you a sinner. It was my sin that was responsible for your death. I have often done the evil that you forbid and have failed to do the things that you have commanded. Forgive me, Lord, for the sake of Jesus, my Savior.
Pastor: It was indeed our sins that nailed our Savior to the Cross. But those very sins also were conquered when he rose again on Easter morning. He lives, truimphant over sin, death and the devil. You are forgiven. Come now and partake of the lamb's high feast.
People: Alleluia. Amen!

The Consecration

The Pax
Pastor: The peace of the Lord be with you always.
People: And also with you.

The Communion
The Hymns
Anthem(s)

The Thanksgiving
Pastor: Oh give thanks to the Lord, for he is good.
People: And his mercy endures forever.

The Benediction
Pastor: Now God the father who lovingly created you with his
      hand,
      God the Son, whose living hands now extend in love to
      you,
      and God the Holy Spirit who holds you ever near;
      May that God bless you and keep you,
      May his face shine on you and be gracious to you,
      May he smile upon you
      And give you his peace.
People: Amen. Alleluia!

The Recessional Hymn *(Suggestions)*
"I Know That My Redeemer Lives"
"Lift High the Cross"

The Postlude

Appendix

Hands — *A Word Study*

1. the **hand** of the Lord
   vengeance of God visited upon someone
   1 Samuel 5:6, 7

2. to pour water on one's **hand**
   to serve the person
   2 Kings 3:11

3. to wash one's **hands**
   denotes that the person is innocent of manslaughter, when the murderer is not known
   Deuteronomy 21:6, 7

4. to kiss one's **hand**
   an act of adoration
   Job 31:27

5. to fill one's **hand**
   to place one into the priesthood to consecrate = (Hebrew) to fill the hand *Judges 17:5, 12; 1 Kings 13:33*

6. to lean upon one's **hand**
   the mark of familiarity, superiority
   2 Kings 7:2, 17; 2 Kings 5:18

7. to lift one's **hand**
   to take an oath *Genesis 14:22*
   posture for prayer and blessing
   Leviticus 9:22

8. to lift up the **hand** against
   to rebel *2 Samuel 20:21*

9. to give one's **hand**
   to grant peace,
   to swear friendship
   to promise security
   to make an alliance
   2 Kings 10:15

10. the right **hand**
    Latin = dexter

ambi = both
ambidextrous = "two right hands"
denotes power, strength
the direction south
   left = north
the accuser commonly stood at the right
   hand of the accused in court
Psalm 109:6; Zechariah 3:1
to be at one's right hand also,
   to the contrary, means to defend,
   protect, support
Psalm 16:8; 109:3

11. God's right **hand**

all the effects of his omnipotence
Exodus 15:6

12. to sit at the right **hand** of God

place of honor and power
Psalm 110:1

13. left **hand**

Latin = sinister
evil

14. to stretch or spread out the **hand**

gesture of mercy
Isaiah 65:2; Proverbs 1:24

15. to put forth the **hand**

to kill someone *1 Samuel 24:10*
to steal *Exodus 22:8, 11*

16. by the **hand** of God

by the power of (Holy Spirit)
1 Kings 18:46

17. laying on of **hands**

ordination or consecration
1 Timothy 4:14
establish judges or magistrates
Numbers 27:18
confession of sins *Leviticus 1:4*
on the accused to signify that he was
charged with guilt of his blood
Deuteronomy 13:9

blessing *Mark 10:16*
conferring of the Holy Spirit *Acts 8:17*

18. God's **hand**

eternal purpose, executive power
Acts 4:28, 30
bounty and goodness *Psalm 104:28*
mighty power to preserve and defend
John 10:28, 29
His corrections *Judges 2:15; Psalm 32:4*
His help *Psalm 74:11*
His favor *Luke 1:66*

19. man's **hand**

power *Proverbs 3:27*
possession *1 Kings 11:31*
advice *2 Samuel 14:19*
tyranny *Exodus 18:9*
work *Acts 20:34*